THE
MAKING OF AMERICA
SERIES

HAMTRAMCK
THE DRIVEN CITY

D1065687

Night time in the city highlights the holiday decorations that were popular for many years.

THE
MAKING OF AMERICA
SERIES

HAMTRAMCK
THE DRIVEN CITY

GREG KOWALSKI

ARCADIA

First printed 2002.
Reprinted 2003.

Published by Arcadia Publishing,
an imprint of Tempus Publishing, Inc.
2 Cumberland Street
Charleston, SC 29401

Printed in Great Britain.

Library of Congress Catalog Card Number: 2002104294

For all general information contact Arcadia Publishing at:
Telephone 843-853-2070
Fax 843-853-0044
E-Mail sales@arcadiapublishing.com

For customer service and orders:
Toll-Free 1-888-313-2665

Visit us on the Internet at http://www.arcadiapublishing.com

CONTENTS

ACKNOWLEDGMENTS

The author would like to express his gratitude to the Hamtramck Public Library and Director Tamara Sochacka for supplying background material and allowing unlimited access to the library archives. Also, thanks go to Irene Namiotka Jordan for sharing her memories of growing up in Hamtramck and to Mrs. Martha Violet Kowalski for her memories of St. Francis Hospital. Grateful appreciation is also extended to *The* (Hamtramck) *Citizen* newspaper and Publisher Karen Spang for use of its file photos. And finally, the archives of the Hamtramck Historical Commission were an invaluable source of information.

The Hamtramck High School baseball team went undefeated in 1928 to win the City of Detroit and State of Michigan Interscholastic Baseball Championship.

Introduction

Founded in the wake of the American Revolution, Hamtramck remained largely unknown for more than 100 years as a dusty farming community on the edge of Detroit, Michigan. In 1910, the town took a new direction with the opening of John and Horace Dodge's auto factory. Within a decade, Hamtramck had become a bustling city. By 1930, it had a population of 56,000 in an area of just 2.1 square miles, making it one of the most densely populated cities in the United States.

Polish immigrants made up the majority of this growing population. In a sense, it was the quintessential immigrant story. These "huddled masses" typically arrived in the United States with little more than what they were wearing and a steamer chest stuffed with their belongings. In a short time, they saved enough to buy homes on tiny lots. Like so many others, they came seeking a better life. After centuries of repression by the Russians, Prussians, Austrians, and Germans, the Polish immigrants hungered for democracy. They embraced the democratic process and quickly began seeking public office. By 1922, when Hamtramck finally incorporated as a city, the Poles were the controlling influence, molding the city into one of fiery politics, gritty urbanism, raucous entertainment, and an intense spirit of living.

They weren't alone. Even as the sounds of heavy industry faded, and the Polish Americans were pulled away from town by the lure of the spacious suburbs, Hamtramck maintained its persona as an immigrant community. From Hamtramck's earliest days, African Americans provided a constancy to the fabric of the community. As it attracted droves of immigrants nearly a century ago, these days Arabs, Bangladeshis, Bosnians, Serbians, and others still find the city an attractive place to settle.

It's been a wild ride between then and now. Hamtramck's saga is filled with the drama of big business tycoons, Communist plots, notorious gangsters, labor goons, corruption of staggering proportions, and destructive political feuds. Hamtramck is driven by industry as well as high emotions, but just as greed and a lust for power drove some "Hamtramckans," so did the desire to build solid homes in a decent community.

This is a story of strong family values, deep religious beliefs, compassionate and landmark educational programs, and an incredibly rich social structure. It is also a story of intriguing and affluent characters, of the corrupt and the charismatic, as well as the honorable and the high-minded. Above all, it is a story of extraordinary people.

Before the giant sewer was built, Conant at the viaduct would turn into "Lake Hamtramck" after a heavy rain. That didn't bother the neighborhood kids a bit.

1. BUILDING THE FRAME

"Who?"

That's the answer most people, including many Hamtramckans, give to the question, "Who was Colonel John Francis Hamtramck?" Historians note that he is probably the least known significant figure of the Revolutionary War. Those who do know the name think it is Polish since Hamtramck has been synonymous with the Polish people for so many years. In fact, Colonel Hamtramck died long before the Polish immigrant influx to Hamtramck in the early twentieth century.

Jean Francois Hamtramck was born in Quebec, of Belgian and French Canadian descent, on August 14, 1756. His father, Charles David Hamtramck, had emigrated to Canada from Luxembourg just seven years earlier. Charles made a simple living as a wig maker and barber. In 1753, he married 20-year-old Marie-Anne Bertin, a French Canadian, and they had five children in all. Only Jean Francois and his sister Marie-Catherine survived infancy.

History swirled around the Hamtramck family. They lived in troubled times in a troubled land. The French and Indian War had broken out two years before Jean Francois's birth, and in 1757, the British captured Quebec. We can only imagine the impact of the subsequent British occupation on Jean Francois. The British rule was oppressive, forcing many French Canadians to flee. Some settled as far south as Louisiana, where they became known as the Cajuns. In 1760 the British also captured Montreal, and by 1763 the final treaties were signed, leaving Canada firmly in British hands. It is not certain how these events affected the Hamtramck family, but many residents rankled under British rule. One account states that Marie-Anne Hamtramck, as a French Canadian, loathed the British.

More certain is the care Jean Francois received from his parents. He was well educated for the time, enough to read and write in English and French, and he had some knowledge of Latin. He must have shared his mother's dislike for the British because it didn't take him long to join forces with the United States when the Revolutionary War broke out in 1775. The war came close to home for the young man when Benedict Arnold led a contingent of soldiers into Quebec and captured the small fort at St. Jean, north of what later would become the border of New York. Although a minor and short-lived victory, as Arnold and his troops quickly withdrew, it was also a sign that the British were not invincible. In

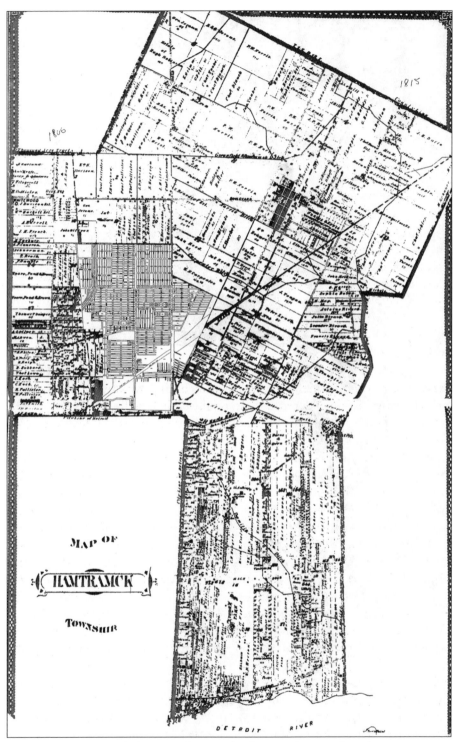

The map of Hamtramck for 1876 shows its borders stretching up from the Detroit River to the county line (Eight Mile Road) and from Woodward to the Grosse Pointes.

September 1775, Hamtramck joined the American forces and quickly fit into the military structure. He was immediately made a commissary, gathering supplies for the troops.

It was a difficult but critical job, and Hamtramck did it well. He attracted the attention of senior officers, formed some valuable alliances, and was soon promoted to captain. Unfortunately, he also made some powerful enemies, including Moses Hazen who had been placed in charge of the Colonial forces raised by Congress to fight in Canada. Hamtramck made the mistake of befriending an enemy of Hazen, and was ultimately demoted to lieutenant and shipped off to a regiment that was later captured. Once released, Hamtramck retreated with the American forces when they were forced out of Canada in June of 1776.

A month later, Hamtramck was in Philadelphia, relaying his experiences to the Continental Congress. By August, a grateful Congress approved his promotion to captain, even though, in the young bureaucracy of the United States, Hamtramck actually had three different dates of appointment to the rank of captain. The most consequential date must have been November 21, 1776, the official date assigned to new officers of the 5th Regiment. It was while dealing with Congress that Hamtramck referred to himself for the first time as John Francis, not Jean Francois.

Hamtramck distinguished himself throughout the Revolutionary War, witnessing action in a wide range of areas, including Yorktown, where General Charles Cornwallis surrendered and essentially ended the Revolutionary War. But peace was only the beginning: The fledgling United States still had to deal with the presence of the British in North America.

Today, the image of the early United States Army is one of citizens valiantly taking up arms against the ruthless and oppressive British. In reality, much of that was true, but conditions for the American troops were often abysmal. Hamtramck, with his experience as a commissary, in charge of procuring food and goods for the troops, knew that well. Pay for the soldiers was sporadic. Consequently, the loyalty of the troops was often tenuous. Conditions worsened as the war dragged on. Desertions became common, and even the officers had to fight bureaucracy to maintain their standing. Hamtramck was well respected as a capable leader, a little rigid, perhaps, but fair. Described as a short and plain man, he made it a practice to ride at the head of his troops on the largest horse he could find. The result was a comical appearance that prompted some unflattering references to his appearance. Nevertheless, Hamtramck fared well with his men, his peers, and his superiors.

Following the end of the Revolutionary War, the young United States was a fairly fragmented collection of often unharmonious neighbors. Much of the army had been disbanded, and the frontier region, out toward Ohio, was just barely under United States control. Under the terms of the agreement that ended the war, the British were supposed to recognize America's boundaries. Nevertheless, they remained in the western wilderness, inciting the Native Americans to harass the Americans, who were pushing westward, establishing settlements in Native American territory. In 1783, Hamtramck was promoted to brevet major and saw action in the west fighting these tribes. He was twice commended by George Washington for bravery.

In 1787, the Northwest Territory was formed from land ceded by the British. This vast tract covered an area that later would become the states of Michigan, Ohio, Indiana, Wisconsin, and part of Minnesota. It was an attractive area that invited settlement, but was fiercely protected by the Native Americans. The British occupation of Detroit further complicated matters, and in the late 1780s, Washington received reports that the British were getting ready to launch an attack on Louisiana, still controlled by the Spanish. In 1790, Washington commissioned Lieutenant Colonel Josiah Harmar to lead a campaign against the Indians and put an end to the warfare. Things didn't go well. Harmar was defeated while advancing on what is today Fort Wayne, Indiana. In response, General Anthony Wayne put together a new army to defeat the Native Americans.

Captain Hamtramck was promoted to lieutenant colonel and assigned to a Second Sub-legion of Wayne's force. General Wayne built Fort Defiance, which today is the city of Defiance, Ohio, and moved east on the Maumee River toward Detroit. On August 20, 1794, Wayne's troops ran into a force of Native Americans in a tract of forest that had been ripped apart by a tornado. Wayne quickly executed a charge, while simultaneously sending a force around to the rear of the Native Americans to cut off a retreat. Colonel Hamtramck commanded a flank in the operation. The Native Americans scattered in disarray, and General Wayne had won the critical Battle of Fallen Timbers. This victory neutralized the Native Americans and cleared the way for the United States to take control of Detroit. The Native Americans, disheartened by the lack of support they sought from the British, signed the Treaty of Greenville the following year, granting the southern and eastern portion of Ohio to the United States.

That still left the pesky British to deal with. By this point, Detroit was already nearly 100 years old, although early Native American settlements found in nearby Flint date back some 10,000 years. These early settlers were the ancestors of tribes that were later recognized as the Ottawa, Huron, Menominee, Miami, Mascouten, Chippewa, and Pottawattami. Little is known of the prehistoric settlers, but early explorers came upon impressive remnants of their presence, such as a 20-foot-tall mound, about 200 feet wide and 300 feet long, near present Fort Wayne, on Detroit's southwestern side. The first explorers had reached the Great Lakes region by 1610. Etienne Brule had been sent by Samuel de Champlain to explore the area and determine if there was a water route to the Orient. Although Brule was illiterate, he left accounts that would help Champlain craft maps of the area and identify possible barriers to further colonization. In 1634, Jean Nicolet followed with further explorations of Michigan. Jesuit missionaries also had a strong presence is the area. Fr. Jacques Marquette, in particular, is noted for establishing settlements at Sault St. Marie and St. Ignace in northern Michigan, but Detroit was Michigan's first real town.

In 1763 Parent's Creek was the site of the battle between Chief Pontiac and British troops. Renamed Bloody Run, it is now in Elmwood Cemetery, once a part of Hamtramck Twp.

Founded on July 24, 1701 by Antione de la Mothe Cadillac, Detroit was established due to the European rivalry between the French and British. The French arrived first and established Detroit, which comes from the French term for "the strait," at the narrow part of the river between Lake St. Clair and Lake Erie. The French wanted to control access to the rich resources of the area, such as furs traded by the Native Americans. Cadillac envisioned Detroit as a true French city, but few people took up the invitation to settle on farmlands along the river. Still, Detroit became the largest French settlement in Michigan.

The antagonism between the French and British across North America grew more intense as the British sought to establish settlements, while the French were fur trading with the Native Americans. Warfare broke out in 1754, in the somewhat misnamed French and Indian War, which pitted these two allies against the British. The British had superior firepower, and in September 1760, captured Montreal, ending the war. France turned over all lands to the west to the British. In November 1760, the Royal American Regiment arrived in Detroit and took possession of the fort built by the French.

Throughout the Revolutionary War and afterwards, the British kept control of Detroit, as well as other forts in Michigan. They were reluctant to give up the trading outposts, which supplied money to the Crown. The young American nation was too weak to force the British out, but once again, events in Europe had effects that echoed in the United States. The British and French were again at odds in Europe, and the British saw it in their best interest to placate the United

States and preserve trade by withdrawing. Those circumstances encouraged the British to sign the Jay treaty in 1794. President Washington desperately wanted to avoid a new war with the British, so he sent John Jay to England to negotiate a new treaty that would clearly establish the United States's borders. Although the treaty was bitterly opposed by many Americans, it succeeded in averting war. Part of the treaty called for the British to leave the forts they held within the boundaries of the United States, as recognized by the treaty that ended the Revolutionary War, including Detroit.

General Wayne was ordered to accept the fort from the British. He suffered from gout, however, and was unable to go to Detroit. Instead, he ordered Colonel Hamtramck to act in his place. Unfortunately, Hamtramck was detained in Maumee, Ohio, so 65 United States soldiers, under the command of Captain Moses Porter, marched into Detroit to accept the British surrender. On July 11, 1796, the British flag was lowered and the British troops departed.

Detroit was now an American city, but many of the residents still loyal to the British were not happy with that turn of affairs and crossed the river into Canada. Detroit's population suddenly declined, but not for long. French traders moved back into the area and the town was too well situated to fail. It quickly became a shipping center. General Wayne was placed in command, but his health continued to worsen and he died within a year. Colonel Hamtramck was ordered to succeed him.

The young United States Congress wanted to exert real control over the area. In 1798, most of Michigan, Ohio, and Wisconsin were organized in one county named after General Wayne. This locale was subdivided into four townships: Detroit, Mackinaw, Sergeant, and Hamtramck. In 1800, most of the territory in Wayne County was split off. Over the next 18 years, the boundaries shifted numerous times as the whole former Northwest Territory was divided and subdivided into the state of Ohio and separate territories.

As for Colonel Hamtramck, he had married Marie Josepte Edeline Perrot in 1790, while stationed in Kentucky. They had two children, Julienne and Henriette. Unfortunately, his wife drowned while crossing the Wabash River in 1796. A year later, Hamtramck married Rebecca Mackenzie and fathered two more children, John Francis Jr. and Alex. His second wife was the sister of the explorer Sir Alexander Mackenzie. John Jr. would go on to a distinguished military career, graduating from West Point and becoming a colonel in a Virginia regiment in the Mexican-American War.

Colonel Hamtramck settled comfortably in Detroit, building a wooden house with two fireplaces on Jefferson Avenue, facing the Detroit River. This property remained standing until 1898. Hamtramck brought his mother and stepfather from Quebec to live with his family, but the arrangement didn't last long. In 1803, Hamtramck was ordered to establish a fort at the mouth of the Chicago River. Sadly, on April 11, 1803, he died. Hamtramck was buried in St. Anne's Church cemetery, where fellow officers placed a slab over his grave with the following words:

Sacred to the memory of John Francis Hamtramck, Esq., colonel of the first United States Regiment of Infantry and commandant of Detroit and its dependencies. He departed this life on the 11th of April, 1803, aged 45 years, 7 months and 28 days. True patriotism, and a zealous attachment to rational liberty joined to a laudable ambition, led him into military service at an early period in his life. He was a soldier even before he was a man. He was an active participator in all the dangers, difficulties and honors of the Revolutionary War. And his heroism and uniform good conduct procured him the attention and personal thanks of the immortal Washington. The United States in him have lost a valuable officer and a good citizen, and society a useful and pleasant member. To his family, the loss is incalculable. And his friends will never forget the memory of Hamtramck. This humble monument is placed over his remains by the officers who had the honor to serve under his command—a small but grateful tribute to his merit and his worth.

Years later, Hamtramck's body was exhumed and reburied in Mt. Elliott Cemetery on Detroit's near east side. In 1928, the weathered plaque over his grave

On May 26, 1962, Colonel Hamtramck came "home." His remains were removed from Mt. Elliott Cemetery in Detroit and reburied at Veterans Memorial Park, in a special ceremony.

site was restored and reinstalled. In 1962, Hamtramck was moved again, this time to what has become the city of Hamtramck, where he was reburied at Veterans Memorial Park.

At the time of Hamtramck's death in 1803, Detroit was barely more than a collection of wooden structures clustered alongside the river. But it was growing. In 1802, it was incorporated as a city, governed by a board of trustees. They passed ordinances, including some specific requirements for dealing with fire. Everyone had to have their chimneys cleaned every two weeks between October and April, and every four weeks throughout the rest of the year, or face a $5 fine. If the chimney caught fire, the fine was doubled, and everyone had to have a barrel of water and buckets at hand. The wooden buildings, tightly packed together, proved a disastrous combination despite the fire regulations. On June 11, 1805, a spark supposedly dropped from a town baker's pipe and landed on some straw near what is now Shelby and Jefferson in downtown Detroit. In minutes, the whole area was ablaze, and soon the entire town was ashes. All but one of the town's 300 buildings were destroyed.

Rebuilding began immediately, and Hamtramck Township, which boxed in the much smaller Detroit, prospered. French farmers settled along the valued riverfront, establishing the unusual "long-tailed patrimonies," or inheritances. These became more familiarly known as ribbon farms. The narrow, but deep,

Records of Hamtramck Township are scarce. Even the names of these township officials have not been preserved.

farms stretched up from the river for long distances. The farm of Antoine Boyez, for example, was about 3.5 acres wide by 40 acres deep. Others were even more extreme, as little as 1.5 acres wide by 34 acres deep. This arrangement allowed more people to have access to the Detroit River, which was becoming key to Detroit's growth as an inland port city and later as an industrial powerhouse. It also guaranteed everyone a stable source of water. Plus, with hostile Native American tribes roaming the area, it made it easier for the farmers to signal each other in case of danger.

Detroit began to set the pattern for its own future—at Hamtramck's expense. In 1806, Detroit annexed a small portion of Hamtramck Township just north of the original town border. Another annexation occurred in 1813, extending Detroit farther north. Further annexations continued in 1827, 1832, 1836, and so on, regularly until 1926. The final bit of Hamtramck Township, a narrow strip of land just west of Grosse Pointe and Grosse Point Farms, was lost to annexation in 1926, four years after the city of Hamtramck had been chartered.

In the early 1800s, however, the area was still wilderness, deep woods of ash, hickory, and maple trees punctuated by unwelcoming marshes. The core of the area's population clung to the riverfront. Yet, as the population increased, so did the demand for land, and settlers pushed their way up into the forests. Looking ahead, Michigan's governor William Hull and Judge Augustus Woodward, one of Detroit's early officials, petitioned the federal government for a grant of land north of present-day Grand Boulevard. This became known as the Ten Thousand Acre Tract, which was surveyed in 1816 and parceled into 48 lots of 160 acres each and 12 lots of 80 acres each. These were sold for as little as $1.25 an acre to help the growing city and provided enough money to build a courthouse and jail in 1823.

On January 5, 1818, Wayne County was reorganized. The original Hamtramck Township was dissolved and a new Hamtramck Township was created. Nine years later, Wayne County was divided again, this time into nine townships: Brownstown, Bucklin, Detroit, Ecorse, Hamtramck, Huron, Monguagon, Plymouth, and Springwells. This third Hamtramck Township was incorporated on June 14, 1827. The area's population was 2,200, including 1,063 persons in Hamtramck Township. It remained largely wilderness. In fact, in 1831, the residents asked the governor to remove the Native Americans from the area because of their persistent raids.

As the century advanced and the Township grew, the landscape changed. Detroit was becoming a major city, which would inevitably impact Hamtramck. In 1838, the first public school opened on Woodbridge Street in Detroit. In 1839, a waterworks with a reservoir was opened at the foot of Orleans Street. Under control of the city, it was Detroit's first public utility. The first successful sewer was constructed in 1835, when the Savoyard River was enclosed in brick and named the Grand Sewer. It ran from Beaubien to the Detroit River. Detroit's first telegraph line was installed in 1847 between the city and Ypsilanti.

By 1845, Detroit had a population of about 13,000 and was becoming a major American city. Hotels, such as Andrew's Railroad Hotel, churches, shops, and markets were established. Railroad lines cut through the city, some to the annoyance of neighbors. For instance, the Detroit and Pontiac Railroad had its Gratiot Avenue tracks torn up by angry residents because the trains kept throwing off sparks and igniting roofs, and no one wanted a repeat of the great 1805 fire. Although one unfortunate train was forced to back up to Royal Oak after encountering the abrupt end of the line, the railroad simply rebuilt the track. Three years later, the angry residents tore up the tracks again, and the railroad got the message. The tracks were not replaced.

Two key elements in Detroit's growth were the Polish and German populations, which would figure prominently, but quite differently, in Hamtramck's future. The first significant German settlement in Michigan was established in Washtenaw County in 1833. The Germans were primarily farmers, and they also found fertile soil in Hamtramck. The remnants of the German community still can be found in such street names as Brombach, Niebel, and Geimer. They shared space with many of the original French settlers, whose names are still represented in such streets as St. Aubin, De quindre, Conant and Jos. Campau, a name that represents one of Detroit's most prominent early families.

Into this mix entered the Polish immigrants, who would have a profound impact in shaping Hamtramck politically, socially, economically, and religiously for more than a century. But in the mid-nineteenth century, many Poles were little more than refugees. Poland has a rich and troubled past. Natives include Mikokaj Kopernik (Nicolas Copernicus), who first proposed that the sun, not the Earth, is the center of the solar system. During the Middle Ages, Poland's liberal and independent spirit invited the oppressed of all nations to take refuge, making Poland a Nazi target during World War II, especially for its large Jewish population. General Thaddeus Kosciuszko fought bravely for the Americans during the Revolutionary War, but was sadly unable to preserve an independent Poland in the years following the revolution. In fact, Poland was partitioned repeatedly by its neighbors right through World War II.

The Prussians, Austrians, Germans, and Russians feasted on the Polish soil. Many Poles came to the United States to avoid being conscripted into the Russian army in the nineteenth and early twentieth centuries. The oppression extended to all levels of Polish life under rule by the foreigners. Teaching Polish language and history could draw a death sentence. The Germans confiscated land belonging to the Poles and repopulated it with German settlers. In the area of Poland controlled by Austria, farms were divided into parcels of no more than 1.25 acres, which was barely enough to support a family. In addition, all forms of Polish culture, such as theater presentations and art, were forbidden. Anti-Catholic sentiments were also strong, as Poland was a predominantly Catholic land, which cherished its devotion to Masses and a wide variety of religious ceremonies and services.

By the mid-nineteenth century, the stage was set. The strife in Poland seemed unending, and the wealthy United States was calling. The earliest known Poles to settle in the Detroit area arrived in the 1830s. Poles began migrating to America in more significant numbers after the American Civil War. Ironically, many of

Polish immigrants were able to buy their own homes, like this one on Wyandotte Street.

these immigrants came from German-controlled Poland and settled in Detroit because that was where the Germans had settled. By 1870, about 300 Polish families dwelt in Detroit.

At that time, Hamtramck Township was huge. It stretched from the Detroit River to the county line, or Eight Mile Road, in the north, and from Woodward Avenue to the west to the Grosse Pointes to the east. The Grosse Pointes had once been a part of Hamtramck, but split off as independent communities in 1848. The area consisted mainly of farmlands, bisected diagonally from the southeast to the northwest by the Grand Trunk Railroad line and from the north to the south on its western side by the Detroit-Milwaukee Railroad. Some familiar main roads that still exist today are Jefferson Avenue, along the riverfront, Mack, Gratiot, Holbrook, and Norris, which was later renamed Mt. Elliott. Creeks crossed the countryside. Holbrook Creek followed the path of what became one of the major roads in modern-day Hamtramck. A mile or so north, Carpenter Creek would later form the northern boundary of the city of Hamtramck. Connor Creek formed part of the township's eastern boundary, and a small portion remained above ground before being covered over near Van Dyke and Seven Mile in the 1970s. Nevertheless, long gone is the old horse racing track north of Jefferson across from Belle Isle. Just a few blocks west was Linden Park, which appeared to be a beautiful sanctuary adorned with ponds. This was an age before Detroit evolved into an industrial center, a time when Detroit was fostering a reputation as a beautiful city of "trees and fountains."

The area that would become modern Hamtramck, toward the center-west portion of the township, was mainly farmland. Detroit provided a rich source of customers for the farmers' produce. Some of the names of the property holders are familiar yet. DeWitt Clinton Holbrook, who was the Wayne County clerk and founder of the Detroit Boat Club, owned a large parcel of land north of what is now Holbrook and Brombach; W.N. Carpenter owned land to the east. William H. Davison owned a parcel at the northwest section of the township that bordered the Ten Thousand Acre Tract. Even at this time, some of the old ribbon farms remained, stretching north from the Detroit River to past Gratiot Avenue.

Soon, those old patrimonies would vanish, along with the original French settlers who populated them. It was the Germans and Poles, in a strained alliance, who were taking over. In 1870, the Polish community had grown so much that the first Polish parish was established. Originally intended to be named after St. Wojciech, Poland's first Christian martyr, a translation error by the Bishop's office left the church christened St. Albertus. It formed the core of what was soon called "Poletown," a name that has had both positive and negative connotations for more than a century and continues still to stir controversy.

With the new parish established, the Poles immediately left St. Joseph Church, where they had worshiped with the Germans. This change was a sign of the growing tension between the two groups, reflected by the feeling that the German-dominated archdiocese was not sensitive to the local Poles. By 1885, the archdiocese had built St. Albertus Church at the corner of Canfield and St. Aubin, about 3 miles north of the river. While Poles settled around the metro Detroit area, establishing churches, Poletown remained the core of the east side Polish community. A major rift occurred between the archdiocese and the parishioners that culminated in a split of the parishioners. Renegade pastor Fr. Dominik Kolasinski took his followers and formed Sweetest Heart of Mary Parish, just a few blocks west of St. Albertus. Just how seriously the Poles valued their religion is shown in the open rioting that broke out in Poletown. The feud between the parishioners and the archdiocese began in 1885 and lasted nearly 10 years. At its worst, there was fighting in the streets, and one man was shot to death. Eventually, Fr. Kolasinski and his supporters made peace with the church hierarchy. Tempers cooled, and the Polish community and the church continued primarily to grow together.

For the Polish community, the churches were more than places of worship: they were centers of the community, and their growth had a direct impact on the development of Hamtramck. Sweetest Heart, with its magnificent stained-glass windows (honored with an award at the 1893 Columbian Exposition in Chicago), was built in 1889. St. Stanislaus, just south of the present Hamtramck border, was established in 1898. St. Florian, a cornerstone of the Hamtramck parishes, was created in 1907. In or out of church, the Poles were deeply religious. Especially after suffering religious oppression in "the Old Country," the Poles found a deep sense of empowerment in the United States where they had the right to express their faith.

In fact, it seems that the floodgates of contained desire for freedom and self-control burst within them when they reached the States. Here they could practice

Hamtramck School Number 1 stood at Beaufait and Gratiot in Hamtramck Township. (Courtesy of the Burton Historical Collection, Detroit Public Library.)

their faith without being punished, here they could own property, here they did not have to worry about being conscripted into a foreign army, and here they could say what they wanted without fear of reprisal. To a large extent, this may explain why they brought such fierce intensity to many areas of life, including local politics. In Hamtramck, this intensity would be given the opportunity to flourish, for better and for worse, as the years would show.

At the end of the nineteenth century, Hamtramck remained mainly a collection of farms. Few records of Hamtramck Township survive, but we do know some of the local names of the period. In 1837, Peter Van Every was township supervisor, Elia Jeruck was clerk, and Dennison Rose, Henry Vaches, and Jacques Campau were assessors. Francis Ruard was "treasurer of the poor." Current street names provide some insight into the past. Moran was derived from one-time township supervisor Charles Moran. Nall, a street in the village of Hamtramck, was named after Detroiter James Nall, who owned property in the area. He also christened Norwalk Street, named after the town in Connecticut where his wife was born. Nall's son was named Edwin. Charles Faber and J. Niebel were early Hamtramck officials and Abram Caniff was a Detroit official. Mitchell was a relative of Joseph Campau. Campau's wife was named Adelaide DeQuindre. Lumpkin was named after a judge in Georgia who was a relative of a local person. William Burger, George Commor, and John Berres were village trustees while John F. Klinger and Charles Geimer had served as village presidents. Whalen was named after Barney Whalen, a one-time police chief.

Even in its township days, Hamtramck was plagued by a drainage problem, and indeed, drainage, sewers, and water supply would remain a continuous issue to the people of Hamtramck through to the present. The problem was a reflection of the town's rapidly growing urbanization. In 1856, the Hamtramck Iron Works opened the first blast furnace west of Pittsburgh. In 1866, the Detroit Body Works was established on Clay Avenue. In 1868, the Hamtramck Street Railway Company was created and operated a horse-drawn trolley originally down Chene and Canfield Streets. This firm would be purchased by the Detroit City Railway Company in 1873. There are also accounts of a Hamtramck steam railway that connected Hamtramck to the old Norris village, near Mt. Elliott and Nevada, about a mile north of Hamtramck. A single engine and car traveled from Denton to Seven Mile Road, crossing Jos. Campau, Carpenter, Conant, Davison, and Mound, up until 1891.

By 1871, the Detroit Stove Works, on the edge of the Detroit River in Hamtramck Township, was one of the area's major businesses, employing 1,300 people and building 700 types of stoves. At the same time, the Peninsular Brewing Company nearby was producing 14,000 barrels of beer a year. Many more breweries would dot the Hamtramck landscape in the years ahead, including some established by the Poles, who brought a fondness for the drink with them to the United States. An old letter shows that John Nett was treasurer of Hamtramck Township in 1900, and Christopher Kraft was appointed the township's first postmaster on April 5, 1899. He operated the postal service out of his business, the Kraft Restaurant and Grocery Store, on Jos. Campau near Council and Dan Streets. It was known as the Kraft station until 1905 when it became the Hamtramck station.

However, while these were signs that Hamtramck was growing in population and urbanization, it was also shrinking. Hamtramck had absorbed Gratiot and Grosse Pointe townships, as well as Norris Village, but Detroit was expanding steadily and the pace of annexations of the township by Detroit was increasing. In 1901, the residents took steps to establish the independent nature of the town by forming the Village of Hamtramck. At that point, Hamtramck had 500 residents and was still a rural hamlet. One of the most prominent buildings in town was still the Old Dolland Farmhouse, at the southwest corner of Jos. Campau and Holbrook, the site of the Hamtramck Town Center shopping center parking lot. Mrs. Dolland died in 1937 at age 97, and at the time was considered Hamtramck's oldest resident.

Despite its name, the Detroit Stove Works was located in Hamtramck Township and was one of the township's leading employers. This ad from about 1870 showcased some of its models.

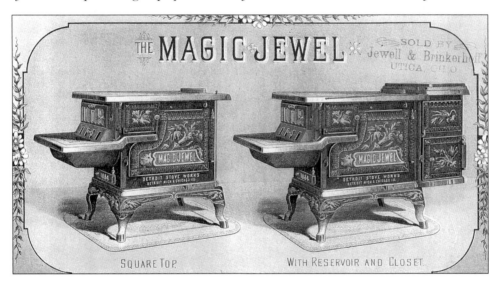

On August 26, 1901, the first village election was held. Anson C. Harris was named village president, having received 116 votes. Henry M. Jacobs was elected clerk; Henry Krauss was named assessor; John Heppner was treasurer; and trustees were William Hawkins, Ernset Oehmko, Henry Mueller, John Segrist, John Berres, and Martin Wojcenski. Most were German: only Wojcenski bore a Polish name. It would be another 10 years before the Poles would begin the great influx into Hamtramck.

The first order of business for the new council, which met in a house on the southwest corner of Denton and Jos. Campau, was to organize the city operations, and, significantly, to draft a village map. A map of the Village of Hamtramck from 1904 shows it to be a much smaller affair than the township. Hamtramck Township still existed at this point, but as a separate entity. The village was more compact and municipally independent from Detroit and the Township. Physically, the village was changing rapidly as farms were being replaced by streets. Familiar streets, such as Goodson, Belmont, Trowbridge, Danforth, and Dyar, were already in place. Other streets that existed at the time have either been renamed or reformatted. Nall eventually became Gallagher, but only ran from Caniff to Carpenter. Holbrook and Carpenter Creeks still existed, and most of the streets were just dirt roads. The majority of the village's population was clustered at the south end of town, toward Poletown and the Polish community that centered on Chene Street in Detroit.

The southern portion of the village was also the site of the Beth-olem Jewish cemetery that served the local Jewish community. Covering a mere 2.5 acres, the first burial there took place in 1871. Eventually, 1,100 people would be buried in the cemetery before it closed its wrought-iron gates for the last time in 1948. By 1915, there were about 35,000 Jews in Detroit, most of whom lived around Eastern Market near Russell and Gratiot a few miles to the south in Detroit. Just a few years later, many of the Jews began an exodus to northwest Detroit, then beyond to Oak Park, Southfield, and West Bloomfield.

In 1901, village officials were occupied with the transformation of Hamtramck into a "modern" town. The chief order of business at the village council meeting held on November 4, 1901 was to consider holding a special election to approve an $88,000 bond "for the purpose of constructing water works for the

These were typical of the buildings along Jos. Campau in the early part of the twentieth century. Similar ones remain standing.

The Hotel Grunewald was located at Smith and Jos. Campau, on the city's far south side, in about 1900.

introduction of water into the said village, supplying the inhabitants thereof with pure and wholesome water for the extinguishments of fires and for the ordinary and extraordinary uses of the inhabitants thereof."

Further business discussion centered around constructing sidewalks along the streets. It was during this period that Jos. Campau became the city's principal street, and the half-mile section of Jos. Campau between Holbrook and Caniff would grow into one of the leading shopping districts in the state. In 1904, however, Jos. Campau was made up of little more than a series of grocery stores and saloons—especially saloons, such as Munchinger's, and watering holes owned by J.P. Kaiser, A.P. Schroeder, A. Buhr, M. Kulczynski, J.C. Adams, L. Becker, and F. Bohn.

Hamtramck was developing into a cityscape following the lead of Detroit, which was expanding and gaining prominence as a manufacturing city. The opening of a railroad tunnel under the St. Clair River between Port Huron and Sarnia, in Ontario, Canada, connected rail lines directly to Detroit, making it a transportation and shipping hub. Manufacturing plants sprang up along the riverfront. Railroad tracks, warehouses, docks, and factories formed a barrier between the riverfront and city beyond. Gone were all but the smallest vestiges of the old ribbon farms. Detroit also became a strategic center for manufacturing railroad cars as well. In 1892, the Michigan Car Company, founded in 1864, merged with its main competitor, the Peninsular Car Company, along with several other manufacturing firms, to form the Michigan Peninsular Car Company. This made Detroit the leading manufacturer of railroad cars, with some 9,000 workers producing as many as 100 cars a day. Detroit's resources, location, and industrial affinity would make it ideal for the growth of another type of car.

North of the river, downtown Detroit was taking on a form of a major modern city. Skyscrapers, while not comparable to the mammoth structures to come in the decades ahead, sprouted upward, and by the turn of the twentieth century, Detroit had a skyline. Even Belle Isle, once a wilderness, was transformed into a pleasurable place to take a carriage ride. In 1889, a bridge costing $300,000 was constructed to the island. The wilderness had been tamed.

Detroit was crowding into Hamtramck Township and boxing in the village of Hamtramck. Next door to Hamtramck, Highland Park had been incorporated as a village in 1889 with a population of about 400. In many ways, this small community would mimic the development of Hamtramck well into the twentieth century, before taking a widely divergent path. Like Hamtramck, it too eventually would be completely surrounded by the city of Detroit and develop into an urban town with strong ties to the auto industry.

It would be the car that would drive Hamtramck into the most remarkable period of its history so far. The reason for that could be summed up in two words: Dodge Main.

The Lawnicki & Jurkiewicz business was located on St. Aubin around the turn of the century. There is no record of what type of business it was, but the Jurkiewicz family also opened a funeral home in the city.

2. Starting the Engine

Enter the auto.

As the twentieth century arrived, Detroit was well positioned to become the auto capital of the world. The infrastructure to support heavy manufacturing was available. Financial institutions and capital to support new businesses were in place. Plus, the port setting in the heart of the Great Lakes provided ready access to huge amounts of resources needed to build cars, such as iron ore and coal for foundries.

In 1899, Ransom E. Olds built a factory to manufacture cars on East Jefferson. It burned two years later and Olds moved his operations to Lansing, the state capital, about 90 miles northwest of Detroit. Detroit's first taste of the auto had been satisfying. Even as Olds was leaving town, David Dunbar Buick, of the Buick and Sherwood Plumbing Co., found that enameling bathtubs was not nearly as interesting as building cars. So, he founded the Buick Auto-Vim and Power Company and began producing autos.

Around the same time, the Packard Automobile Company moved from Ohio after it was bought by a group of Detroiters. Henry Ford, the man most closely associated with car manufacturing, built his first car in 1896. Ford, a gifted mechanic, understood how to build cars and would later revolutionize the industry by combining his car design with the rapid construction process offered by the assembly line. At the turn of the century, however, Ford was tinkering with forming manufacturing companies as well as focusing on building racers. It was one of those, the "999," that propelled him to greater exposure when legendary racer Barney Oldfield drove the car to victory in a highly publicized auto race in Grosse Pointe in 1902. As a result of that win, coal dealer Alexander Malcomson pulled together a band of investors to bankroll Ford to form the Ford Motor Company.

And there were others. Henry Leland was chiefly responsible for founding the Cadillac Motor Car Company in 1902. William C. Durant, a one-time errand boy, formed a partnership with J. Dallas Dort to form the Durant-Dort Carriage Company. Durant in particular was so successful that he was asked by Buick's financial backers to assume control of that company. He did and made it a major success. Later, he acquired the Oldsmobile, Cadillac, Oakland, and several other

John and Horace Dodge (Horace at far left) posed in the first car delivered to them by the Production Department at Dodge Main in November 1914. The photo was taken in front of the Dodges' house in Detroit, a few miles west of the Hamtramck plant.

car companies to form the General Motors Company, ultimately creating the Goliath of auto companies. Walter Chrysler, Charles Kettering, William Knudsen, and the six Fisher brothers also played key roles in the early development of the auto industry. There were others as well, but they are virtually forgotten today, such as the Reo, Hudson, Chalmers, Hupp, King, and Maxwell car companies.

In these early years of the auto industry, the car companies were not important to the village of Hamtramck, which was still somewhat remote, at the northern fringes of Detroit. All that would change in 1910 when brothers John and Horace Dodge decided to open a factory inside the village at the southeast border of the town. The impact of that decision would shape the future of the city for 70 years and leave what would perhaps be an indelible imprint.

John and Horace Dodge were the sons of a machinist who taught them his craft in Niles, Michigan. In 1892, the brothers found jobs in Windsor, Canada, at the Dominion Typographical Company. There they picked up experience learning precision tools used in die-making and patterns. When that company failed, the Dodges moved to another firm. Along the way, they had invented a ball bearing mechanism for bicycles, which they leased to the company. That company also failed, and the Dodges were offered their choice of machinery in lieu of the royalties they should have received from the invention. The brothers moved to Detroit in 1900, and opened a machine shop manufacturing, among other things, "simple, compound triple and quadruple expansion marine and stationary engines."

Their business prospered and they began to branch out, producing parts for the new auto companies, including Olds and Ford. They even bought stock in Ford, which would fuel their own ambitions to build an auto plant. The Model T generated much money for the Ford company and its investors. In 1909, the Dodges received $180,000 in dividends from the Ford Motor Company. In 1910, the dividends amounted to $200,000. The Dodges' sales proved so lucrative, the brothers outgrew their downtown Detroit plant and sought a site to build a new one. They selected a large tract of land in Hamtramck. Still largely rural and offering room for expansion, Hamtramck was close to Detroit and critically important railroad lines cut through the area. In June of 1910 the foundation for the forge was dug, and within six months the plant was operating.

The new plant had an almost old-world charm in its design. The guard house had a Spanish-style, half-cylindrical, tile roof and the streetlights were ornamental with curved embellishments. The brothers had separate offices on the second floor of the administration building, which fronted Jos. Campau. John's office occupied one end of a long hallway, while Horace's office was at the other. Their secretary's desk was directly in between. By all accounts, the plant was an immediate success, but the Dodges had a better idea. They weren't content to be just a supplier, they wanted to get into the auto manufacturing business.

Granted, the brothers employed some unusual business practices that wouldn't find much favor today. During the miserable summer heat, the Dodges would bring in sandwiches and barrels of beer for the workers, which must have done wonders for quality control. Nonetheless, they also adopted some impressive and progressive practices, such as establishing a $5-million fund to aid sick and injured workers and the widows of employees. The Dodges tried to provide good lighting and ventilation in the factory. They also experimented with paying the workers their $3-a-day wage in cash instead of check to put an end to the employees' habit of stopping at the local bars to cash their checks. The workers objected, plus handling all that cash became a problem, so the practice was soon dropped.

During this period, John had become a vice president at Ford, but he resigned in August of 1913, complaining that he was tired of being controlled by Henry Ford. Besides, the Dodges knew they would soon be in direct competition with Ford, as they planned to build their own car. When they made the formal announcement of their manufacturing plans, they were immediately flooded with applications from would-be dealerships: 22,000 by the end of 1914, the first year their new car hit the streets. Sales were slow the first year of production, with a mere 214 touring cars produced. The following year, Dodge introduced a two-passenger roadster, which increased employment at the plant to 7,000 as sales skyrocketed. By 1915, they topped 45,000 units and the Dodges were making significant improvements to their products, such as better fuel systems. The models sold for about $800, which put them just within reach of most buyers, although a bit more expensive than the Model T.

More production required more room, and the original 20 acres of floor space were expanded to 72 acres in 1916. The plant began to take on huge dimensions, eventually encompassing more than 30 separate buildings, rising up to eight stories. The twin assembly buildings on the plant's south side were 100 feet wide by 1,080 feet long. Designed by leading architect Albert Kahn, and made of reinforced concrete, the buildings were built to last a thousand years. In fact, they lasted 70 at the most, but proved incredibly difficult to demolish in the 1980s.

However, when the buildings were rising, the future seemed to offer only growth and prosperity, and indeed, that was the case for the Dodge company and the people of Hamtramck, but not for the Dodge brothers. Both died in 1920. While visiting the North American Auto Show in New York, John Dodge was stricken by the influenza epidemic that was returning after sweeping around the world in 1918 and 1919. Despite prompt medical treatment at the posh Ritz-Carlton Hotel where the Dodges were staying, John Dodge died at 10:30 p.m. on Wednesday, January 14 at the age of 55. The next morning, the men at the Hamtramck plant were gathered together and given the news, which was received with stunned silence. Eleven months later, Horace fell ill. His condition worsened steadily, and he died on December 10 of cirrhosis of the liver, while visiting Palm Beach, Florida. He was 52.

"The Man Who Drove Around the World" (third from left) stopped by Hamtramck to meet with city officials at the city offices on Jos. Campau and Grayling in 1925. His name was not recorded. Others pictured are assistant city attorney Stephen Majewski, and Councilmen Stanley Jankowski and Casimir Zarzyka. At far left is Joseph Czarnecki, who founded Liberty State Bank. At far right is Stanley Sporney.

In 1914, members of the Hamtramck Fire Department posed with their ladder truck at what may be the first fire station, a two-car garage at the Detroit Lumber Company. The fire department dates back to 1857 when the "Hamtramck Spouters" were organized in Hamtramck Township. In 1883, a firehouse was built at Grandy and Gratiot.

Both the Dodges lived large, relishing their wealth. They were unbowed by Prohibition, and frequently would go on drinking excursions around town. They perceived themselves as down-to-earth folks despite their wealth, and would drink with the plant employees at the burgeoning number of bars in Hamtramck. That and their factory kept them as deeply involved in everyday life in Hamtramck as they wanted to be. They maintained homes in fashionable Grosse Pointe and the exclusive Boston-Edison district of nearby Detroit, but their reality for the most part was a universe away from the typical Hamtramck home. Still, they had more influence on the people of Hamtramck and the city itself than anyone else to that time.

Here's why. In 1910, Hamtramck had a population of 3,559. By 1920, the population was 48,615. Virtually all of the phenomenal growth could be attributed to the Dodge brothers' factory, which affectionately was known as Dodge Main throughout its existence. The $3-a-day wage wasn't much, but it was steady and more than most places paid. Henry Ford was offering $5 a day at his plant in Highland Park, just a couple of miles northwest of Dodge Main, but you only got that pay rate if you worked there a year. Also, Ford made meddlesome demands on the workers' lifestyles so that they would save money and attend night school. The Dodge brothers weren't concerned about reforming society. They just wanted to build cars.

Even before Hamtramck became a city, there was no escaping taxes, as is shown by this 1915 delinquent tax bill for a resident of the village of Hamtramck.

In the space of a few years, Hamtramck was no longer a dusty farm town. By 1906, there were 22 miles of streets, about half of which were accompanied by water mains. Telephone service was also introduced to the village in that year. Three years earlier, electric wires had been strung across town. The city was becoming a densely urban area. Builders were quick to capitalize on the rapidly growing population, and simple frame houses were thrown up at a furious rate. In 1901, there were 252 houses in the village. By 1914, that number had grown to 2,061 houses, and six years later, the number topped 5,730. Most were placed on 30-foot-wide lots barely 70 feet deep. More than 80 percent of Hamtramck's houses were built between 1915 and 1930. Few had indoor bathrooms: most had outhouses in the backyard or toilets in the garage. There was no central heating: instead, most houses were heated by wood stoves in the living room. During the winter, family activities were mainly confined to this warmer area of the home, which would be sealed off from the rest of the house by French doors. Even today, a few examples of these doors can be found in Hamtramck houses. Closet space was minimal (which remains a bane to modern Hamtramck residents) because people had less clothes to store. Between 1930 and 1945, all the remaining outdoor toilets were moved inside to pantry space or to newly added-on bathrooms that almost invariably were located off the kitchen. While such an arrangement would likely cause a seizure in a modern designer, that was a practical layout then because it allowed all the main household plumbing to be grouped in one area.

Surely no house in Hamtramck from this early period remains in its original state, as all have undergone some degree of modernization. In 1920, a simple frame home for many residents was an American dream, one made much more profound by the circumstances of the residents. And who were these people?

Almost all Hamtramck residents were Polish immigrants, drawn to Hamtramck to work in Dodge Main and, to a lesser extent, the Ford plant in Highland Park. At that time, public transportation consisted of streetcars, which, while adequate, were not always convenient. Factories were often located right in residential neighborhoods, or neighborhoods grew up around them, so the workers could live near where they worked. Many Dodge Main employees walked to work. Similarly, schools, stores, churches, and all manner of buildings were clustered together. Into the 1970s, Wyandotte Street, for example, had a factory, houses, a high school, and stores all within the length of one city block. It

In 1913, a resident complained about the assessment of his lot in a carefully worded letter to the village assessor.

was an urban planner's nightmare with no thought of zoning, but it worked because the people who lived there appreciated it as a vast improvement over what they left behind in Poland, and they prized what they had.

By the early part of the twentieth century, more than half of the Polish Americans in Detroit owned their own homes. Property ownership was a matter of pride. Renting was undesirable, but acceptable because not everyone could afford to buy a house. Maintaining private property would come to characterize Hamtramck in later years when visitors to the city invariably would remark about how the residents would routinely sweep the streets in front of their homes.

Most of the Hamtramck residents came either directly from Poland, or migrated from another area of the country, such as the coal mines out East or north from Poletown in Detroit. Like most immigrants, they tended to settle together in groups where not speaking English would be less of a hindrance. They shared customs and traditions and, often, family ties. They also had a strong work ethic and a tough constitution, which allowed them to work in the grueling atmosphere of the factories like Dodge Main. Factory workers have never had an easy lot. The work was repetitive to the point of being mind-numbing. The hours were long and the conditions deplorable. It was noisy, dirty, dangerous, and hot. In summer, temperatures would climb over 100 degrees. And in the foundry, it was even worse, as workers baked in the oven-like heat. Conditions like these persisted well into the twentieth century, and former employees can still remember wildcat strikes called when the heat became overwhelming and

Even before the 1920s, the assembly line at Dodge Main already was in full production.

workers were desperate to get into the air. Local bar owners recall how workers would stop in at 7 a.m. and drink enough to dull their senses for the morning so they could withstand the conditions in the plant. Then it was back to the bar at lunch, or after their shift to unwind.

Nonetheless, as tough as conditions were at Dodge Main, the factory wove its way into the fabric of life in the city. Of course, not every Hamtramckan worked in Dodge Main, but its presence was felt in other ways. Small businesses depended on it either by directly supplying the plant or relying on the paychecks the workers drew from the company. Little stores sprouted up on almost every street corner and the number of bars grew to staggering proportions. There is no clear record of the exact number, but it's said that Hamtramck had more bars per capita than any other city in the United States. Prohibition was barely more than an inconvenience, as many residents realized the Roaring Twenties icon of bottling gin in their own bathtubs. Many village trustees were saloon keepers, and this supposedly helped lead to Hamtramck's incorporation into a city.

By the late "teens," Hamtramck's population was approaching 48,000, almost all comprised of Polish immigrants. Most of the village officials were Germans, who looked on this influx of immigrants with growing concern. Given the history of German dominance of Poland, Germans and Poles seldom felt more than toleration for each other. The Polish immigrants had little experience with democracy, but they were learning. In the United States, they discovered the power of the ballot box and their equality as voters.

What happened during this period may be a local urban legend, but because it has persisted so consistently through the decades, it is worth relating. According to the account, the German village leaders were becoming alarmed at the growing influence of the Polish immigrants and feared losing control to the Poles. A group of German village officials supposedly contacted Detroit officials and struck a deal: they would work to merge Hamtramck with Detroit on the condition that they retain control of the town (although how that could have been done is questionable). When the local Poles heard of the plan, they were outraged and began a movement to incorporate as a city. Under Michigan law, a city cannot annex another city, so incorporation would protect Hamtramck from its big neighbor. There probably is some truth to this story, since there was extant animosity between the Poles and Germans, and Detroit had been whittling away at Hamtramck Township for more than a century.

Wherever the truth lies, it is indisputable that the residents did vote to incorporate as a city on October 10, 1921, by a nearly four-to-one margin, 870 votes to 240. Technically, Hamtramck officially became a city on January 21, 1922, when the governor signed the legislative act incorporating it as such.

The original city charter described the boundaries, which place the city in the northeast central area of Detroit. It covers 2.094 square miles located at 42.22 degrees north latitude and 83.03 degrees west longitude. Peter C. Jezewski, a popular pharmacist who operated a pharmacy at Jos. Campau and Belmont, was elected the city's first mayor. The new mayor and council, elected in April of

On a warm Sunday afternoon, members of St. Peter A.M.E. Zion Church, one of Hamtramck's most venerable African-American churches, prepare to picnic at Belle Isle.

1922, reflected the city's changing ethnicity. The council was made up of Andrew Templeton, Casimir Plagens, Dr. James L. Henderson, and Walter Gaston. Joseph J. Mitchell was city clerk and Walter Merique was treasurer. Justices of the peace were Stephen Majewski and Walter J. Phillips.

Dr. Henderson was an African American and he wasn't the first black Hamtramck official. Just prior to incorporation, Ordine Tolliver, a prominent African-American resident, served on the village council. While Hamtramck was predominantly French and German in its early years, becoming overwhelmingly Polish later on, African Americans have played a significant role in the town from its earliest days. Census figures for 1827 listed seven African-American people among the 1,063 residents. Over the years, Hamtramck's population of African Americans has consistently remained at about 12 percent. In the early years as a city, it wasn't unusual for white Polish immigrants to rent space in homes owned by African Americans. They shared space at a time when the rest of the country was almost entirely segregated. Black and white children played together and went to school together. African-American policemen were employed by the city from its earliest years, in addition to working as doctors, lawyers, and businessmen.

Many noteworthy African-American residents made a substantial difference in the community. Among them was Haley Bell, who co-founded Bell Broadcasting System in 1955, the home of WCHB-AM and WCHD-FM radio stations. For years, Iris Butler was known as "Hamtramck's Angel of Mercy" for her commitment to the community, which spanned from 1918 to 1965 and included being the city's Health Department nurse. Yvonne Myrick and Amanda Dumas also have taken places as dedicated Hamtramckans. Myrick became the first African-American president of the city employee's union and a member of the Hamtramck School Board. Dumas is also remembered fondly by many for her dedication in helping others in a variety of ways, including serving on the Hamtramck Historical Commission.

Relations between Hamtramck's white and African-American residents weren't without problems. Until the 1960s, segregation persisted at the restaurant counter in at least one store on Jos. Campau. The devastating urban renewal lawsuit of the 1960s created some bitter animosity, which will be related later.

In 1922, diversity was not the main concern: crafting a city was. Hamtramck was set to become a major powerhouse economically and politically in the state of Michigan. Despite the deaths of the Dodge brothers and lackluster leadership by their heirs, the plant continued to grow. Over the 1920s, the factory was enlarged several times to cover an area of about 3.3 million square feet. In 1925, sales reached 200,000 cars even though the Dodge heirs sold the plant to a group of New York investors, who, in turn, sold the factory for $170 million to Walter P. Chrysler in 1928. This was an era of prosperity for Chrysler and Hamtramck, for when Dodge Main prospered, so did the city. The plant ultimately would supply about 25 percent of the city's tax revenue. Over the years, Chrysler would regularly pay its taxes in advance to bail the city out of its routine financial shortfalls. And there were many.

Hamtramck's history has traditionally followed two parallel paths. The first traces the route of city government, which often proved to be riddled with

Store signs abound along Jos. Campau, looking north from Belmont Street around 1958. The P.C. Jezewski drug store, owned by the city's first mayor, is at far right.

corruption. The second centers on the social development and community strength that allow the city to survive the worst disasters engineered by city hall, at the same time serving as points of pride for a community of amazing resilience. Even in Hamtramck's village days, it developed a reputation as a wide-open city. Within Detroit but separate from it, Hamtramck provided a convenient haven for Detroiters, even prominent ones, who could appreciate the anonymity that Hamtramck offered. During Prohibition, Hamtramck was a popular watering spot where drinks flowed freely. Paddy McGraw's brothel attained a legendary reputation. It was situated at the far south end of town right next to the railroad tracks, and men from as far away as Toledo and Flint would catch a train that would drop them off and pick them up literally at the front door. Inside, owner Patrick "Paddy" McGraw apparently had learned a lesson from Henry Ford (although the allusion surely would send Ford spinning faster than a crankshaft) by adopting an assembly line policy for the ladies to share space in the small rooms with their customers. Paddy was a civic-minded soul as well, sponsoring sports teams and actively participating in the annual Goodfellows newspaper drive to provide toys to needy kids at Christmas.

This kind of schizophrenic morality was common in the period. People engaged in all manner of illicit behavior, while being otherwise upstanding citizens, and the police could generally be bought off. The situation reached a critical stage in 1924 when a convoy of illegal liquor coming into Hamtramck was intercepted by the Michigan State Police. Mayor Jezewski was implicated, charged, convicted, and sent to Leavenworth prison for two years, and he wasn't the last mayor to serve time for corruption. By the mid-1920s, vice was so rampant that the Wayne County prosecutor asked the governor to send in the state

This is believed to be A. Buhr's bar at about 1905. There were numerous saloons throughout Hamtramck village. The numbers would grow enormously with the opening of Dodge Main.

police to take control of law enforcement. In 1923, the state police conducted nearly 200 raids in the small city. Most were for gambling and illegal liquor. On one small street block, Charest between Holbrook and Evaline, six houses nearly side by side were raided.

While Hamtramck's corruption was serious, it was not unique. Aside from the growing gangster activities in big cities across the United States, even small towns had severe problems. A year before the state police moved into Hamtramck, martial law was declared in the small town of Mexia, Texas, and the Texas Rangers had to take control. The governor of Pennsylvania sent their state police scrambling to close down speakeasies and brothels. Prohibition itself had become a threat to society. In general, Hamtramck's crime in the Roaring Twenties was self-contained and rather tame compared to the big city that surrounded it. A few serious gangsters operated out of Hamtramck, such as Chester LeMare, the so-called "Racket King of Hamtramck," but he was shot twice in the head by a supposed friend while living in a house in Detroit. The notorious Purple Gang also frequented Hamtramck spots from time to time. Members of that ferocious group were imported to Chicago to carry out the St. Valentine's Day Massacre for Al Capone. But for the most part, the Purples operated in Detroit. They, like so many honest people, were drawn to Hamtramck as a refuge to quietly enjoy a drink or two, or a dozen. Given the living conditions of the city at the time, it is in fact remarkable that more serious crime didn't occur. One area where it was more obvious, however, was in juvenile delinquency.

Delinquency rates for boys age 7 to 16 were substantially higher in Hamtramck than Detroit between 1927 and 1931. Typically, the kids were involved in larcenies. In retrospect, that's hardly surprising considering the living conditions of these kids. Many did not speak English, so they had great difficulty in school. Many dropped out. Further, it was not uncommon for teens to quit school to go to work to help support the family. Work at the factories was often sporadic. Model changes and economic downturns would lead to layoffs, and there were no economic cushions for these folks who lived from paycheck to paycheck with no unemployment compensation in between. Many people drank too much, which strained families to the breaking point. Old newspapers frequently tell tales of young men who hung themselves in their houses after being laid off or who strayed drunkenly onto the railroad tracks where they were killed by trains. The trains were a lure to the errant youngsters as well, and were frequently targets of theft. Many young people (and adults) would steal fist-sized chunks of coal for the home stoves, and later, the coal-fueled furnaces that replaced the stoves. While life in Hamtramck was better than in Poland, it was hardly a paradise.

There was help, which came from three principal sources: churches, social organizations, and later, schools. These three groups were cornerstones of the community, and were in many ways far more important to the people of Hamtramck than the often dysfunctional city government. Each was distinct and quite different, but all in their own way improved the lives of the residents. Although almost all Hamtramckans had close ties to the church in Poland before

Stately St. Florian Church was designed by noted architect Ralph Adams Cram, and has changed little since it was built in the mid-1920s. This cornerstone parish was created in 1907.

they immigrated, the earliest Polish churches were in the Poletown area of Detroit. As the population began to move north into the village of Hamtramck, the archdiocese ordered the organization of Hamtramck's first Polish parish, St. Florian, in 1907. The first Mass was celebrated in the fall of that year in a rented building on Jos. Campau near Berres Street. Fr. Bernard Zmijewski was appointed first pastor, and he immediately did a survey of the area to determine how many parishioners the fledgling church would have. He found only 74 families, but that was enough to go forward with plans for building a church. He immediately began organizing the parish, and formed a committee to locate a permanent site for a church. Two residents donated plots of land measuring 300 by 220 feet to serve as the foundation for the new church, which was poured in the spring of 1908. It would be another 15 years before an impressive Gothic building, designed by architect Ralph Adams Cram, would be built on the site.

With the growth of the area largely due to the Dodge factory, a school was constructed in 1909 alongside the church. Within two years, the school had an enrollment of 477. Accordingly, St. Florian's parish expanded enormously. By 1919, the school had 2,500 pupils. That increased to 2,853 by 1923 and St. Florian was the second largest parish in the diocese of Detroit. Like the city of

Hamtramck, St. Florian was booming. Debt-free and with $23,000 in the bank, it was time to erect a church building that would remain to this day a crowning achievement of architecture, as well as a spiritual commitment to and by a community. With a 200-foot spire, St. Florian is still Hamtramck's most prominent landmark, visible from 2 miles away along the I-75 freeway.

But a parish is more than bricks and steel: it is a distillation of a community. More than 10,000 people attended the consecration of the church in 1928. Many of these people had sacrificed what little they had to donate money to help pay for the church. Some mortgaged their homes to raise money, and some craftsmen even helped build the structure. In return, they found the security and comfort of their faith held not just in a building, but in the entire infrastructure of the organized church. St. Florian embodied the deep faith that was instilled in them in Poland. Many parents who could barely support their families sacrificed everything they could to send their children to the parochial school for a Catholic education.

Religious ceremonies were key elements in the lives of the parishioners. The Catholic traditions of Midnight Mass on Christmas Eve, Lenten fasts, and Stations of the Cross services, May procession, receiving ashes on the forehead on Ash Wednesday, First Holy Communion, confessions, and more played themselves out with unrelenting regularity without losing importance for decades. Some people even went to church every day.

With Hamtramck's population skyrocketing after 1910, even St. Florian could not meet the needs of all the Catholic residents. Our Lady Queen of Apostles Church was formed in 1917. Two years later, St. Ladislaus parish was founded about a half-mile north of St. Florian. In 1922, Holy Cross Polish National Catholic Church was established by a group of dissident Poles who split with the church hierarchy.

Clearly, religious feelings were strong in Hamtramck, spanning all cultural and ethnic groups. Some years later, in 1937, Immaculate Conception Ukrainian Catholic Church was formed at the north end of town. This parish serves as a reminder that Hamtramck wasn't populated entirely by Catholic Poles. The Ukrainians belong to the Eastern Rite. Also, Corinthian Baptist Church, founded in 1917, has served the African-American community since then. The same is true of Macedonia Baptist Church, which was founded in 1922 and continues to operate today and St. Peter Zion African Methodist Episcopalian Church, which was founded in 1909. From 1908 to 1925, a Jewish temple occupied two sites in Hamtramck, first at the Beth-olem Cemetery grounds and later on Wyandotte Street. These places of worship helped give strength and support to the people in those often troubled times when there was no job security, Social Security, or health insurance.

While churches tended to the spiritual needs and, to some extent, the social needs of the community, a variety of social and community organizations also arose. The Polish Falcons, founded in 1887, focused on athletics. The Hamtramck Indians traced their roots back to 1890, primarily acting as a political organization into the twentieth century before turning to more social concerns. The Polish

41

National Alliance predated the Hamtramck Indians, and was founded to help educate and integrate the Poles into American society. Other groups that operated in Hamtramck over the years have included the Polish Roman Catholic Union, Polish Legion of American Veterans, the Alliance of Poles, Hamtramck Polka Boosters, Polish American Century Club, Polish Army Veterans Club, General Thaddeus Kosciuszko Club, and the Legion of Polish Veterans of World Wars. St. Anne's Community House also provided service.

Above all, one organization shares an extraordinary history and impact: Tau Beta. Formed in 1901 by four high schools girls—Eloise Jenks, Hildergarde Meigs, Margaret Snow, and Marian Stinchfield—Tau Beta would have a profound effect on the lives of thousands of Hamtramckans. In its earliest years, the organization was basically a sorority for fairly well-to-do teens, but it grew and soon began to do charitable activities, such as sewing and selling items to raise money for the needy. They also began cooking meals, which they delivered twice a week to shut-ins and the poor nearly a century before the Meals-on-Wheels program of today, with great success. In 1915, noting the needy immigrant population in Hamtramck, the Tau Beta ladies opened a kitchen in association with the Babies' Milk Fund clinic operating in town. That first year, they made 566 home visits. The following year, they made 1,297.

Tau Beta operated out of a modest flat at 159 (now 3213) Hanley Street, called "the house with the light" because of the porch light that burned nightly. Most likely, the ladies were somewhat appalled at the surrounding conditions. In their official history, published in 1938, they describe the then-village as one of dusty lots, "but no playgrounds." The village government was described as unreceptive to the needs of the overwhelmingly uneducated and foreign-born people around

Thousands of Hamtramckans were proud to carry Tau Beta membership cards.

Over the years, the Tau Beta Community House sponsored a variety of activities for adults and kids, including the "Novelty Parade," which resembles a scene from The Little Rascals.

them. Tau Beta began offering cooking and sewing classes, then music and gardening classes. Neighborhood children were taken on picnics to far away Palmer Park in north Detroit. In August of 1918, Tau Betan Miss Marion Miller took 11 young girls for a vacation at a cottage at distant Lake Orion for what must have been for them an excursion to the wilderness.

The need for Tau Beta's service was great. During the influenza epidemic of 1918, Tau Betans were pressed to the limit, calling doctors and making physician referrals. They also helped women find jobs and even served as consumer advocates, in one case helping a woman get the coal she had paid for from a reluctant company that refused to deliver it to her. By 1919, Tau Beta was a serious social organization offering a wide variety of programs for children and adults ranging from English classes to a weekly community clothes wash. Tau Beta even operated a day care from 6:30 a.m. to 5:30 p.m., five days a week. The organization began to receive major contributions, including an $11,546 gift from the Dodge family in 1921. Several sets of reference books were donated, forming the basis for the future Hamtramck Public Library. New books began to arrive at a steady pace from Hamtramck High School. Tau Beta began to conduct a variety of recreational programs at the Hamtramck Public Schools. They also sponsored music and theater productions at St. Florian school and later at Keyworth Stadium. In 1928, Tau Beta moved across the street to a much larger headquarters housed in an impressive Tudor building, which included a theater.

Tau Beta officially left Hamtramck in 1958 when it was finally deemed that its services were no longer needed, but even today, many residents still have their Tau

Crowds of people turned out to pose for this picture on October 30, 1916, shortly after Hamtramck High School opened between Wyandotte and Hewitt Streets.

Beta membership cards and some irreplaceable memories. Even as the organization was wrestling with some of the severe social problems of Hamtramck, the public schools also saw that there were needs that went far beyond what could be supplied in the classrooms.

The Hamtramck school district grew slowly over the years. In 1901, there was one school in the village of Hamtramck. Holbrook School, on Alice Street, began as a one-room frame schoolhouse built in 1896. It was expanded several times over the years, and remarkably, remains open today—spanning more than 100 years of continuous use. With the immigrants came a sharp demand for new schools, and between 1917 and 1924, several more buildings were either added or renovated: Hamtramck High School, which opened in September 1915; Whitney School; Pulaski School; Carpenter School; Kosciuszko; Dickinson School; and a vocational school. In addition, Holbrook School was expanded to a three-story brick structure. Other buildings would be added later.

In the 1920s, Hamtramck educators were faced with the challenge of trying to teach many students who couldn't even understand what they were being told. Some spoke a little English. Some spoke none at all, but their problems extended far beyond language. Many of these children were desperately poor and in need of basic heath care, which they had never received in their lives.

In 1923, the Hamtramck school board realized that something significant had to be done to incorporate the influx of students and integrate them into American society. In a stroke of brilliance, the board hired Maurice Keyworth as new school superintendent. Keyworth was a graduate of the University of Michigan and a Midwesterner who seemed to be as far removed from the children of Old Poland as a person could be. Yet he understood the unique challenge that Hamtramck presented and knew how to work with the administration. Keyworth had 15 years of experience in education before coming to Hamtramck, and in that time had developed a progressive view of education that was far ahead of its time. In Hamtramck, he was allowed to implement his methods with almost complete freedom. Like an artist given a free brush, he transformed the Hamtramck education system into one of the most progressive in the nation. Methods he pioneered were adopted by school districts across the nation and are considered standards of operation today. His philosophy was put forth in the School Code adopted in 1920, which stated:

> The purpose of public education in Hamtramck shall be to develop individuals who can live successfully in a democracy. Successful living means that (1) they must be able to see the problems in their own lives, and in social life; (2) they must be able to solve these problems successfully; and (3) they must will to take the necessary steps to achieve the solution. An analysis of successful living shows that there are six major fields of problems. These are: (1) health; (2) ethical character; (3) citizenship; (4) vocational activity; (5) home membership; and (6) recreation. In each of these fields it shall be the policy to make the child acquainted with the present-day problems, with a knowledge of the achievement and methods of solution developed by man in the past, and with the needs and possibilities of the future. The methods used to achieve these objectives shall be those which will develop in the child (1) the ideals of worthy individual and social purposes; (2) powers of self-direction, self-appraisal, and self-control; and (3) the desire and ability to work cooperatively with others in the solution of social problems.

Massive and stylish, Copernicus Junior High School was built in 1931 and continues to be used today as Hamtramck High School.

45

Translated into practical terms, the School Code set the pattern for turning the students into productive citizens. To do that, Keyworth understood that the children had to learn English. But even more fundamental, the children had to be physically able to learn. He instituted health clinics in the schools and all children received annual health checkups. For the first time in their lives, many children received dental care. Basics like nutrition, good health habits, and personal hygiene were taught to the children. And they were vaccinated for smallpox and diphtheria, which, while not common in the 1920s, still occurred sporadically. Children with health problems were given special treatment and facilities, such as a swimming pool for use by kids with orthopedic problems. Arrangements were provided for children with tuberculosis and heart ailments. Continuing with his policy of inclusiveness, Keyworth established a "Psychological Clinic" for children with behavioral problems and state agencies were called in to help provide psychiatric services for kids with more serious special needs.

In the classroom, Keyworth instituted progressive teaching methods that included what would be called block scheduling today. Children were placed in small groups that focused attention on specific areas and were encouraged to recognize problems, solve them, and evaluate their solutions. These methods are virtually the same as those used by many schools today.

Keyworth believed that education extended beyond the classroom. He sent teachers and school nurses to visit homes to meet with parents. Keyworth

Dr. Maurice Keyworth stands at far right in this photo in 1927. Keyworth turned the Hamtramck public schools into some of the finest in the nation. He stands here as a member of the Hamtramck Centennial Jubilee Committee, formed to mark the 100th anniversary of the creation of the third Hamtramck Township. With him are (from left) A. Buczynski, V. Smith, H. Karbowski, L. Koscinski, E. Tyszka, C. Zarzyka, and S. Jankowski.

The first Copernicus Junior High School band practiced outside of the school in June 1932. The exterior of the building has changed little since then.

understood then the modern perspective that, "It takes a village to raise a child." Parents were to be involved in the education of their children. Keyworth instituted school bulletins that were regularly sent home to the parents to keep them informed and involved in the schools. Under Keyworth's direction, adult education classes prospered. English lessons were taught along with citizenship classes. In 1936, more than 3,000 adults were enrolled in evening classes. Plus, a range of vocational programs taught specific trades that proved invaluable to many students later during the Great Depression, when jobs were scarce. And most importantly, under Keyworth, the Hamtramck Public Schools remained financially sound through the worst years of the Depression.

Of course, Keyworth had critics. Then, as now, some viewed teaching techniques that strayed far from basic reading, writing, and arithmetic as experimental and of dubious value. Plus, Keyworth exercised great control over the school administration, including having nearly total control of hiring and firing staff at all levels. This created friction among some staff and administrators who had their own ideas on how the schools should be run.

No one could really argue with Keyworth's success. Hamtramck students who had entered the schools knowing little about America and even less of the English language would graduate with honors, going on to college and taking good jobs. By the mid-1930s, Hamtramck's public schools were attracting national attention and Keyworth was considered one of the leading educators in the nation.

In 1935, Keyworth resigned from the Hamtramck public schools when he was elected state superintendent of public education. Where this would have taken him and how he would have shaped public education in Michigan and perhaps nationally we will never know. On June 22, 1935, Keyworth was killed in an auto accident near Sault St. Marie in Michigan's Upper Peninsula. His car was struck head-on by another. Even though he had officially left the city, his body was brought back to lie in state at Hamtramck High School. Only days earlier, he had given the commencement address to the graduating class of Hamtramck High School. His subject was "Goals and Education of the State of Michigan." No one then could realize that the speech would be historically significant, if only for being the last he would give in Hamtramck. The 1935 school bulletin emotionally summed up the feelings of many:

> Darkest of all years was 1935, because on June 22, the great guiding genius of this institution was removed by death. It came at the time when he, and the schools which reflected his personality, were at their highest point of achievement, and when his sun was still in ascendancy. It came when, after years of labor, he stood on the threshold of official recognition. It came when the hand of reward was extended to place the laurel wreath. It came when the State of Michigan could least afford to lose him, but it came, fortunately, after his efforts had at least shown us the light of day ahead, the door for which we were to emerge from the caverns of financial despair.

Maurice Keyworth is arguably the most significant figure in Hamtramck's history. More than anyone else, he directly and positively influenced the lives of thousands of Hamtramckans. His school system is a source of pride in Hamtramck, as well as an idea emulated by some of the greatest cities across the nation. And he made it work, even as the Great Depression struck with a force that would stun all of Hamtramck.

3. Hitting the Brakes

To the typical Hamtramckan, the events of October 28 and October 29, 1929 meant nothing. The collapse of the stock market in distant New York had no immediate meaning to the people who had no stocks or bonds. They went to work as usual, did their shopping, probably heard the ominous news on the radio, but went to the movies or to see local acting troupes for amusement. Not for long. Soon, the curtain of the Great Depression began to descend, and ultimately, it would land hard.

Michigan in particular was hurt badly by the Depression because of the auto industry. Prior to the Depression, people had been encouraged to buy big ticket items, like cars, on the installment plan and had accumulated a lot of debt. Following the stock market crash, Henry Ford expected sales to drop and reacted by cutting the price of cars in November of 1929, but a measure like that was useless in the face of the economic downturn that was devastating businesses and industry. In 1929, 5 million cars were built. By 1932, that number dropped to 1.3 million. As sales evaporated, so did jobs. Michigan, with its economy so tied to heavy industry, was sent reeling. The unemployment rate in non-farming areas soared to 20 percent in 1930 and a staggering 50 percent by 1932, the worst year of the Depression.

At Dodge Main, which had been expanding since it opened, the situation quickly grew desperate. In 1929, the plant had nearly 30,000 workers who produced about 250,000 cars. In 1932, a mere 28,111 cars were produced. Most of the workforce was laid off. The timing of the Depression was especially bad for Hamtramck. The population in 1930 reached an almost overwhelming 56,268 people packed in an area of 2.1 square miles. The town did not have high-rise buildings, unlike the tenement sections of New York City, which boasted similar numbers. Hamtramck was a flat city built mainly of frame houses, although some had as many as four families in a two-floor structure. Few other communities anywhere attained such a population density, but all that meant was that people could share their misery more closely.

Poles had a difficult time integrating into American society even in the more prosperous years leading up to the Depression. About 15 percent of the Polish population in Detroit relied on welfare, even though it was especially painful for

Hamtramck State Bank was one of the many that didn't survive the Great Depression. The building still stands at Jos. Campau and Council Street, on the city's South End.

the proud Poles to accept aid. For the most part, they preferred to rely on church charities or Polish social organizations for help, but the effects of the Depression were nearly beyond imagination. In 1932, about half of the Polish community in Detroit was unemployed. In Hamtramck, about half of the city's 11,000 families were on welfare by 1932. Losing a job was a devastating blow to a worker. Incidents of suicide and domestic violence increased as pressure mounted on families. Rates of tuberculosis started climbing, as did juvenile delinquency. One notable case was the arrest of two boys who said they were members of the Black Ace Gang, which burglarized more than 20 houses in eight months.

Supplementing the pain of unemployment was the loss of life savings with the collapse of the banks. Many of the immigrants had arrived with little money. They treasured what they acquired. Some sent money back home to relatives in Poland, and everybody saved what they could. In 1929, eight banks operated in Hamtramck with assets of $11.9 million. Most of those banks didn't survive the Depression, and their closing seared into many residents a deep distrust of banks that would last long after the Federal Deposit Insurance Corporation and other banking safeguards were put into place. Until they died, some Hamtramckans refused to ever trust the banks again and kept their money at home. The city government became so desperate for cash that in 1934, the city issued its own scrip in $1, $5, and $10 denominations, which it used to pay employees. These bills later were redeemed for actual U.S. Mint money. Many Hamtramckans today still have the City of Hamtramck bills tucked away in dressers or storage boxes.

Ironically, however, the severity of the Depression had a unifying effect. Survivors of this difficult time still recall that they could take some comfort in that, while an individual was poor, "so was everybody else." You may have had tattered clothes but you would not be teased, since no one's clothes were any better. The suffering people tried to draw some scant comfort from these types of situations.

Soon the city was overwhelmed by applications for welfare. The claims quickly drained the city's resources and, in an attempt to stretch them, families with less than three children were dropped from the welfare rolls. Evictions from homes became common and families were forced to take in relatives, compounding the already overcrowded conditions. People began to go hungry.

Those who did have jobs were hardly better off. Wages plummeted. Auto workers who were making up to $7 a day before the Depression found their wages cut by more than half. Businesses still operating did so with a minimal workforce, virtually working them to death. Dodge Main sped up the assembly lines to the point of inhumanity. Workers who complained were summarily fired. There were plenty to take their places. Even going to the bathroom could be risky, since you might not have a job when you got back to the line. It was a common practice to ply the foremen with gifts as a form of job security, and there was little enough money to buy food for the family, let alone "gifts" for the boss. Work was sporadic and layoffs common. Plus, there was no guarantee a laid-off worker would get his

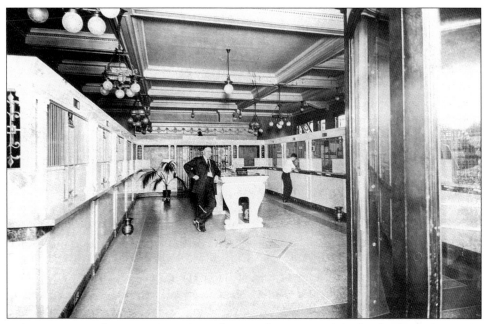

Liberty State Bank on Jos. Campau and Norwalk was one of the few banks to survive the Great Depression. It later moved to Holbrook and Jos. Campau and eventually became a branch of the Huntington Bank.

job back when the lines started up again. Even before the Depression, factory work was hard, but that was magnified by the new economic reality.

Not surprisingly, dissent festered in the hot, dirty, noisy buildings, and talk about unions began to circulate in hushed tones. Such talk was dangerous, for it could get you immediately fired, usually on the pretext of doing "shoddy work" or being insubordinate. Henry Ford was passionate in his hatred of unions. The feeling was mutual at the Chrysler Corporation, which by now owned Dodge Main. The company planted professional spies among the workforce to identify union sympathizers and obtain union membership lists. A "Works Council," essentially a company-formed union in the plant, was supposed to deal with employee concerns. However, it was firmly in the control of management, which packed the voting ranks to favor the company. Workers were angry and frustrated. Attempts to form unions were bitterly and sometimes violently resisted by the companies, and the unions often were at odds with each other. The craft unions looked down on the industrial unions and didn't trust them. Some union leaders, like William Collins, who was sent by the American Federation of Labor to organize the auto unions, openly opposed strikes, the union's principal bargaining tool.

Still, with little or no improvement in various factories, the unions took hold, at least among some of the workers. In early 1935, workers at Dodge Main formed the Automotive Industrial Workers Association. Their first goal was to get management to reduce the nine-hour work day to eight hours. Management responded by threatening to subcontract their jobs to suppliers. The union recognized that the best way to counter the company was to organize the competition so there would be no cheaper alternative available. But organizing was tough. Although President Franklin D. Roosevelt had implemented some labor reforms, including the right of workers to organize, he severely undercut the unions by supporting company-controlled Works Councils. The Supreme

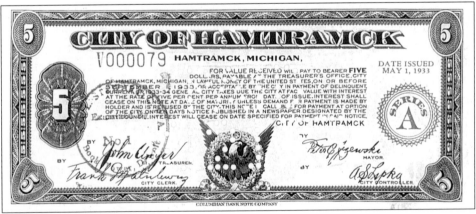

Strapped for cash in the Great Depression, the city issued its own scrip in 1932 and 1933 in denominations of $1, $5, and $10.

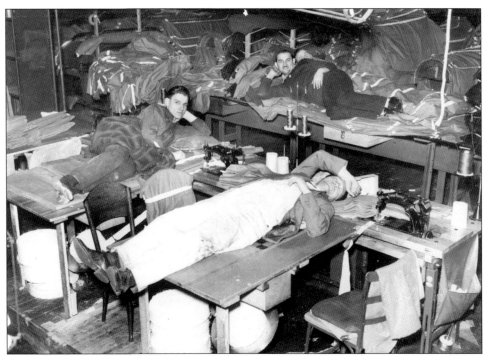

Workers placed makeshift bunks among the machinery at Dodge Main during the sit-down strike of 1937. For the most part, the strike was an exercise in boredom. (Courtesy of Walter P. Reuther Library, Wayne State University.)

Court worsened the situation in May of 1935 by overturning Roosevelt's National Recovery Act, which included the right to organize.

The unions continued to struggle, but remained persistent. In March of 1937, the situation reached one of several historic climaxes. At 1:30 p.m. on March 8, thousands of workers in all nine Chrysler Corporation plants in the Detroit area staged a massive sit-down strike. The tactic paralyzed the plants as the company wasn't able to lock workers out and bring in scabs as replacements. The only way to remove them was to call in the police. But the police didn't want to step in because the strikers outnumbered them and weren't afraid to turn to violence. The strike quickly spread to other industries and an estimated 35,000 workers sat down on the job, while another 100,000 walked the picket lines outside the various businesses ranging from cigar factories to meat packing plants.

For the most part, a sit-down strike was an exercise in boredom. Behind barricaded doors, the workers spent days camped among the machinery, playing cards or checkers, and waiting for something to happen. They were supplied by family members and friends passing food in through the windows. Outside Dodge Main, picketers walked a line 1.9 miles long around the huge plant. Chrysler went to circuit court to get an injunction to get the workers out of the plant. Despite an emotional plea by the union attorney, Judge Allen Campbell

After nearly three weeks, it was over. On March 25, 1937, streams of workers filed out of Dodge Main, ending the landmark sit-down strike. (Courtesy of Walter P. Reuther Library, Wayne State University.)

ruled that the workers didn't have the right to seize millions of dollars worth of property. The workers responded by building stronger barricades at the doors. They weren't going anywhere.

The situation worsened. Bolstered by the court decision, Detroit police began conducting raids at various businesses, forcing the striking workers to evacuate the buildings. The unions remained defiant and planned to hold a massive rally outside city hall. The city council denied a permit for the rally, but it was staged anyway, on March 23, with an estimated 100,000 persons demonstrating in support of the workers. Nonetheless, soon both sides seemed to realize they had pushed the issue to the limit. They agreed to sit down together, this time at the negotiating table, and reach a settlement. On March 25, a cold and snowy day in Hamtramck, the workers evacuated the plants, bringing one of the most significant strikes in labor history to an end.

As the last of the strikers walked out of the plant onto Jos. Campau, about 500 supporters were there to meet them. They marched up this main city road behind men carrying an American flag, a blue and gold UAW banner, and a 75-piece marching band. Two weeks later, Chrysler Corporation and the United Auto

Workers signed a deal. The UAW agreed not to stage any more sit-down strikes, and Chrysler agreed to recognize the union, while not supporting any other group to undermine it.

All of Hamtramck breathed a collective sigh of relief. The *New Deal* newspaper led its story on the end of the strike with "Greater Hamtramck stepped off a keg of dynamite yesterday." The strike had put city officials in a precarious position. On one hand, the city heavily relied on tax revenue from the plant, and Chrysler was generous, making early tax payments. On the other hand, many of those sit-down strikers were residents, and more crucially, voters, and they turned out in huge numbers to support their brothers in the plant. Thousands came out for a rally in front of the plant on Jos. Campau, and there were numerous other rallies. The 95-member police department was put on alert when the strike broke out and officers were assigned to 12-hour shifts. But when it was over, police chief William Berg reported to the council that no serious incidents had occurred and no arrests had been made. The fire department placed five firefighters at the plant while it was shut down. Even the local saloons were put on alert, and all those around Dodge Main agreed not to sell any worker more than "a reasonable amount of liquor."

Another side effect of the strike was that the city was suddenly inundated with applications for jobs from strikers. Hamtramck was also put under pressure by strike supporters who came before the city council and demanded that they provide beds and food for the strikers. Additionally, they asked for a variety of increases of service to welfare recipients. The council responded that the city didn't have any money for increased benefits. Even Councilwoman Mary Zuk, who was long suspected of being a Communist, came under fire—in Polish, no less—when she was berated at a council meeting by a striker for not providing enough aid to the poor.

Zuk illustrated another facet of the strike, and the labor movement as a whole, that put off most city officials: the Communist Party. The involvement of the Communist movement with labor is a long and complicated story that went far beyond Hamtramck, but that had little meaning to most Hamtramckans. The workers toiling under miserable conditions in Dodge Main didn't care much about such politics, but when someone offered support to improve conditions, the workers took notice, even if that ally was a Communist. The Communist Party of the United States was formed in September of 1919, barely two years after the Russian Revolution. Although it was separate and generally rejected by the long-established Socialist Party, which viewed it as too revolutionary, the Communists and Socialists were usually lumped together by the general public as radicals. Business, of course, was horrified by the Communists, who virulently rejected capitalism.

"Bolsheviks," the Communists were called, often in a tone reserved for obscenities. Anti-Communist feelings ran so strongly that at one time, it was illegal to wave a red flag in Michigan. In 1918, Schiller Hall at St. Aubin and Gratiot was bought by the Socialist Party of Michigan, which renamed it the

House of the Masses. It became a gathering place for radicals, socialists, and labor groups. On the night of January 2, 1920, the police pounded down the doors and arrested 200 people as part of a sweeping operation in 32 cities nationwide to arrest 5,000 Bolsheviks. They were to be charged with planning to overthrow the United States government. Two days later, a second raid at the House of the Masses was conducted, leading to more arrests.

Anti-Communist feelings were running high, and other Communist and Socialist groups noticed, including those operating in Hamtramck. The city had its own version of the House of the Masses, the International Workers Hall, at 3014 Yemans, a building that still stands today. The Detroit police Red Squad files indicate that the Hall had been owned by the Communist Party, although the ownership always remained somewhat vague. It was clearly a center of Communist activities and was so for decades. Nefarious plots against capitalists were discussed in the dim reaches of the Hall, but they generally amounted to nothing. For decades, the FBI monitored the activities at the International Workers Hall, which had become a significant center for the Communist Party in North America.

At the height of the Red Scare in 1951, a rally attended by 300 persons was held at the Hall to protest the jailing of John Zydok, who was listed by police as head of the Hamtramck Communist Party. He had been arrested in a raid at the Workman's Co-op restaurant, where he was head waiter. The Co-op was so closely associated with the Communists that for years it was known by its nickname, "Russians." The Zydok protest came only months after the city employees' union asked the city council to require that all city employees sign affidavits that they were not Communists.

While the Communists were shunned, prosecuted, and persecuted, they also persevered, even taking a high profile. Their leader in Hamtramck, George Kristalsky (sometimes spelled Krystalski), ran for office several times, and actually polled a respectable amount of votes: 1,372 votes in his bid for city council in 1939, and finished eighth among 10 council candidates a few years later. In 1934, the Communists mounted a full slate: Krystalsky running for mayor; Richard Ruffini, Michael Laslo (apparently replaced later by George Moszczynski), Cass Bailey, Jennie Romaniuk, and Frank Dziubik for council; Michael Zackler for city clerk; and Emil Sobol for treasurer. Significantly, Bailey was an African American, and had Romaniuk won, she would have been the first woman elected to office in the city. That distinction, however, would go to Mary Zuk a few years later. The Communists ran on a platform, "Against Hunger, Wage Cuts, Fascism and War!" In fact, their campaign was based on a set of progressive proposals that are startlingly familiar today. The 10-point platform demanded the following:

1. A minimum of 75 cents per hour for all factory workers: a 30 percent increase for all those now earning 58 cents per hour. A maximum of a 6-hour day, five days a week. A guarantee of 40 full weeks work a year: $22.50 a week minimum that is a guarantee minimum yearly earnings of $900.00 for all workers in the industry.

ROBOTNICY HAMTRAMCK **Głosujcie na Komunistów**

Przeciwko Głodowi i Faszyzmowi

Na Mayora—

GEORGE KRISTALSKY

Na Konsilmanów—

RICHARD RUFFINI   JENNIE ROMANIUK
CASS BAILEY   FRANK DZIUBIK
GEORGE MOSZCZYNSKI

Na Kasjera—   Na Klerka Miejskiego—
EMIL SOBOL   MICHAEL ZACKLER

(Over)

Vote Communist, the Workers of Hamtramck Against Hunger and Fascism urged in the
1930s. This political handbill was printed in English and Polish.

Workers of Hamtramck **VOTE COMMUNIST—**

Against Hunger and Fascism

For Mayor—
GEORGE KRISTALSKY

For Councilmen—
RICHARD RUFFINI   JENNIE ROMANIUK
CASS BAILEY   FRANK DZIUBIK
GEORGE MOSZCZYNSKI

For Treasurer—   For City Clerk—
EMIL SOBOL   MICHAEL ZACKLER

(Over)

2. Immediate cash relief for all unemployed without any discrimination against Negroes or Foreign-born, at the rate of $10.00 per week for each single person, $15.00 per week for each family of 3 and additional $2.00 per week for each dependent, pending the enactment of UNEMPLOYMENT INSURANCE paid by the employers and FEDERAL Government for all unemployed workers.

3. Free, hot, nourishing lunches in the public schools, clothing, shoes, books and school supplies to all children of unemployed and part-time workers.

4. SOCIAL INSURANCE paid by the industry and government covering sickness, occupational disease, accident, maternity, old age pension, etc. Opening of City Clinic to give sufficient medical attention to the unemployed and part-time workers and their families.

5. No discrimination against Negro workers and immediate hiring of Negro workers to work on all jobs in all departments in the shops.

6. The right of workers to (join) the union of their choice, to elect shops and department committees without fear of victimization. Workers to have the right to strike to enforce their demands regarding wages, hours, conditions and other vital needs of the workers.

7. The abolition of the inhuman speed-up system on the belt, etc. That the City pass an ordinance that it should be unlawful to discharge or refuse employment to any worker solely because he or she has reached an age of 40 or more years, as is practiced by Chrysler-Dodge and other employers in Hamtramck.

8. An extensive program of public works to be started immediately, such as paving all unpaved streets in Hamtramck, grade separations at Conant and Grand Trunk R.R. and Caniff and Grand Trunk R.R., building of sufficient playgrounds and recreational centers in the neighborhoods, eliminating slums and run down houses, especially in the Negro sections.

9. Full union wages to be paid to all workers employed on relief jobs and all public works, such as CWA. In no case less than 75 cents per hour, for no more than 6 hours a day, with 5 days a week. No discrimination against Negroes, foreign-born, women and young workers. Equal pay for all.

10. Absolute prevention of any evictions of unemployed or part-time

workers. Such evictions to be made criminal offenses. All relief allowances to apply without distinctions to race, nationality, religion or political beliefs or affiliations, citizenship or length of residence. Gas, electric, water, fuel and rent to be paid by welfare department to all unemployed and part-time workers.

Pretty ambitious, to say the least, yet not entirely unrealistic. Equal rights for women and African Americans are a given today, but were far from reality in the 1930s. Age discrimination remains an issue even today. The platform also gave a keen insight into the issues that were especially important to people at that time, principally welfare services and an end to the devastating evictions that were especially painful to families.

As a whole, the Communists didn't fare very well. Perhaps the closest they came to attaining any political power was with Mary Zuk. But Zuk, at one point, flatly denied being a Communist. Later, she was less direct in her denials. Regardless, her critics branded her as leftist. In any case, she made history in Hamtramck by being the first woman elected to the city council. Born Mary Stanceus in 1904, she emigrated from the coal mines of Virginia with her family and settled in Hamtramck. In 1922, she married Stanley Zuk, who worked in the auto industry until he lost his job during the Depression. Around that time, Mary Zuk became active in social issues, joining an unemployed workers group.

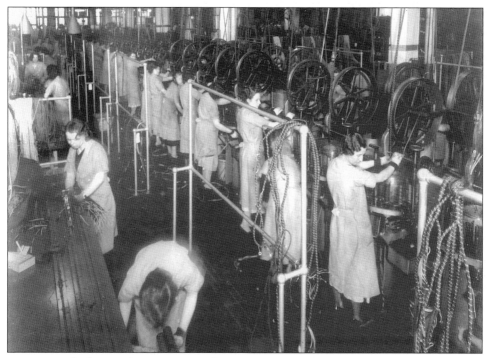

Women worked in Dodge Main, as well, operating machines.

In 1935, she came to prominence by leading an organization called the Committee for Action Against the High Cost of Living, which was made up of Hamtramck women who were struggling to keep their families together while trying to deal with rising costs. Their immediate goal was to get a 20 percent cut in the price of meat. On July 19, 1935, they met at the Polish Falcons Hall in Hamtramck and voted to appeal to local butchers to trim their costs. They refused. A second meeting was held on July 26 at Copernicus School and Zuk, who had played a lesser role in the organization to this point, was made its leader because of her radical stance, calling for a strike against the butchers and picketing in front of their stores. The strike soon spread to Detroit. From the start, the strikers said their target was not actually the stores, which operated at a small profit margin, but rather the meat packers, who controlled the prices by how much they charged the markets, were to blame. But the packers were insulated, while the markets were out on the streets, and those streets were packed with strikers shoulder to shoulder, carrying signs with the legends, "Don't Buy Meat!" and "Force Meat Packers to Lower High Prices."

After a week of picketing, many butchers relented and reduced prices, but the strikes continued when they refused to sign an agreement permanently lowering

With fiery rhetoric, Mary Zuk rose to take the lead of the Meat Strike in 1935. She would later be the first woman elected to the Hamtramck city council. (Courtesy of Walter P. Reuther Library, Wayne State University.)

them. Soon, incidents of violence broke out after a group of 200 strikers attacked the J. Johann Package Company on Mitchell Street with the intent of destroying the meat inside. Four persons were arrested, but released on a promise to report to court the following week after 300 persons appeared at the Davison Police Station and demanded their freedom. Later, the McGraw Police Station was overwhelmed by more strikers seeking to release their comrades. The situation was taking on alarming proportions and the butchers asked, through the National Association of Retail Meat Dealers, that the National Guard be called out. They threatened they would close up shop for good. Spurred by the angry butchers, the police began guarding butcher shops, although they had all closed by about the third week of the strike. Zuk and the strikers responded by holding a mass rally, attended by 5,000 people, at Perrien Park in Detroit. Zuk addressed the crowd:

> We are going to keep fighting until we knock out these politicians.
> Working people don't want to eat bones. We want President Roosevelt to
> give us a country like the Constitution provides. And we working people
> are the ones who can make him and Congress raise our living standards.
> We're going to make him understand he can't kill off the little pigs. And
> when we get through with the meat, we'll start on gas and electricity and
> the sales tax.

The Hamtramck Grocers and Butchers Association responded at a meeting at the Polish Century Club where they vowed to use revolvers and cleavers to defend themselves and their property.

The strikers got little support from the Hamtramck administration. Mayor Joseph Lewandowski labeled them as Communists, although he later apologized for the remark. Still, the strikers were headquartered in the International Workers Hall, a known Communist headquarters. Echoes of the strike began to be felt in Macomb County, and as far as Chicago and Washington, D.C. On August 9, Congressman John Dingell, of Detroit, introduced a bill to investigate the price of hogs. All along, the packers had maintained that the conditions in the Great Dust Bowl in the Midwest were affecting cattle prices. Dingell's proposal went nowhere. Nevertheless, Zuk led a group of women to Washington to meet with President Roosevelt to present their demands for an investigation of their charges of price-fixing by the meat packers. They made it as far as Calvin B. Hoover, consumers counsel in the Department of Agriculture. The women returned to Hamtramck, disheartened. Their cause suffered further blows when the courts issued injunctions against picketing at a meat packing plant, then at 19 butcher stores in Hamtramck. On September 9, the strikers gave up. Said the still defiant Zuk: "We opened the eyes of the nation, when we started. Although we cannot boast of any big reduction in the price of meat, we did manage to lower the cost a little. Not much, but a little."

But it did a lot for Zuk politically. The following year she won a seat on the Hamtramck City Council as the first woman ever to serve. Her strength was with her connection to the people suffering through the Depression. She campaigned for more welfare benefits, union scale wages for those working, protection for unions, tax reductions, and the elimination of "black lists" and "Labor spy agencies." During her brief tenure on the council, Zuk was bitterly attacked as being a Communist, but it wasn't politics that cut her political career short after just one two-year term in office: it was religion.

Zuk went through a highly publicized and bitter divorce that played out in full detail in local press. Her husband had publicly denounced her as neglecting her family. Zuk maintained that he, in turn, had been physically abusive, taken her money, and been an unfit husband. Her political stature drew public attention to the ordeal and, since divorce did not sit well with the overwhelmingly Catholic voters of the 1930s, Zuk lost her bid for re-election. The new administration gave Zuk a job as Water Department commissioner, but a year later, when the department was dissolved, Zuk lost the position. She remarried, left Hamtramck, and slipped into obscurity. While not remembered by many today, Zuk remains one of the most colorful characters in Hamtramck's history.

Despite the lack of support the strikers had received from the Roosevelt administration, Hamtramckans as a whole supported the Democratic Party. Under Michigan's governmental structure, mayors and city councils technically are non-partisan positions, but Hamtramck voters and politicians quickly chose sides. The Republicans were seen as the party of big business and the rich. The Democrats were seen as friends of labor and the poor. Herbert Hoover reinforced that impression with his reluctance to have the government do much to alleviate the hardships of the poor and even the hungry during the Depression, preferring instead to leave that to overwhelmed charities. It didn't take long for Hamtramck to become a solid Democratic stronghold. This was not insignificant.

When Roosevelt was running for president, Hamtramck had a population of more than 56,000 people, almost all of them Democrats. Hamtramckans voted in huge numbers, but this was not always the case. A magazine article from 1921 noted that of the city's population of nearly 50,000, only 6,000 voted. However, the Americanization programs in the schools actually worked, and organizations also helped the Poles tap their seemingly natural propensity for democracy. By the 1930s, it was not unusual to have a 70 percent voter turnout in any election. The presidential election of 1936 was typical: Roosevelt received 15,870 votes, compared with Alf Landon's paltry 842. That was the most lopsided vote for Roosevelt recorded by any city of more than 50,000 in America.

While the meat strikers got a disappointing response from Washington, D.C., the city as a whole fared much better. In 1936, despite being in the depths of the Depression, Washington approved $79,500 to construct a new post office building on Caniff, just east of Jos. Campau. It's interesting to note that shortly after the post office opened, people began complaining that postal service was "worse than ever" with waits of 90 minutes while service windows remained closed. Nevertheless, the building remains an impressive example of Art Deco architecture decorated with three painted panels on its interior walls. The

In the late 1930s, a group of WPA artists produced paintings for the Hamtramck public schools. This is a representation of a post office at the time.

paintings and building were both funded through the Works Projects Administration (WPA), a federal program that would have a major presence in Hamtramck.

The WPA was formed in May of 1935, and was actually a conglomeration of projects created earlier in the decade, designed to provide jobs for the estimated 10 million unemployed at a pay of about $50 a month. It encompassed and replaced the Federal Emergency Relief Administration, the Public Works Administration, and the Civil Works Administration. Those programs created jobs mainly in the construction industry, but the WPA broadly expanded the range of programs to include educational, library, and health service projects, and later, art, theater, music, and literature. It and the related Civilian Conservation Corps, which put people to work in such projects as planting trees, offered a lifeline in the Depression. It wasn't much, but it was something. It was a chance to work again, to collect a paycheck, not a welfare check, and to feel a sense of pride. It was a way to buy food and maybe give up a nickel now and then to see a movie at one of the neighborhood movie houses. For artists and writers who face a challenge making a living in the best of times, it was a godsend. It was because of the WPA that we have some of Hamtramck's early records. As part of the WPA Historical Records Survey, workers laboriously copied the earliest village records word for word from the original ledgers written in longhand, some of which have since vanished.

The post office wasn't the only large-scale project created in Hamtramck by the WPA. Keyworth Stadium, an impressive brick football stadium named in honor of former school Superintendent Maurice R. Keyworth, was built in 1936 behind Veterans Memorial Park, in a project mainly funded through the WPA. It was

Heavy industry backed up the edges of the city. This is the area behind Keyworth Stadium. In the distance is the smokestack of Swedish Crucible Steel Company.

significant enough, and another demonstration of Hamtramck's growing political strength, that President Roosevelt came to Hamtramck to dedicate it on October 15, 1936. Roosevelt told the crowded stadium:

> We have tried to keep people from starving. We have tried to save the homes of the nation. We have tried to restore employment to the people of the nation. My friends, I think that in three years we have come a long way.
>
> But it has been not only the emergency that we have had to cope with. We have been thinking about some of the things that the country needs in addition to food and lodging and that is why a great stadium of this kind appeals to me as one of the things that will last for many years and contribute towards enjoyment and recreation not only for us older people but for the younger generation as well.

Within a week of Roosevelt's visit, delighted Hamtramckans were preparing to rename the street leading to the stadium Roosevelt Street.

The WPA had its detractors. In some cases, jobs were handed out through political favoritism, and conservatives blasted it as a "Make Work" program. Even some unions fought it because they said it undercut the prevailing wages. In December of 1941, the United States entered World War II. The involvement solved the unemployment problem for millions of Americans. In July of 1943, all the WPA programs were ended as America concentrated on the war effort, but while it lasted, the WPA improved the lives of millions. Hamtramck still has some remnants of that era, such as the post office and Keyworth Stadium, plus a collection of more than 50 superb paintings done in the late 1930s and early 1940s by WPA artists for the Hamtramck Public Schools. These turned up in Grosse Pointe Farms in 2000, and were placed on sale by a local gallery. The sale was a sellout, showing that the WPA is not forgotten, and in some ways, prized.

With the Depression, labor strikes, Communists on the loose, tuberculosis, and an undercurrent of political strife, one could easily get the impression that Hamtramck was in constant turmoil. In fact, it was not. Day-to-day activities continued despite the hardships imposed by the Depression and all the other factors that made life tough. But the people were tough as well. They knew the true meaning of family values: that the family would be there for support when all else failed. It was a tradition brought from the Old Country, but not limited to just Poles. The African-American community long ago learned that it had to rely on family, not government, for even the most basic assistance. Only in the 1960s did government begin to offer real support for civil rights. Hamtramck also had a small, but significant, Ukrainian population with its own traditions, language, and family ties.

Through the worst of the Depression, people simply made do as best as they could. By the 1930s, there were plenty of stores around the city supplying what people could buy at prices, for the most part, that they could afford. In 1937, Val Magielski's Victory Market on Conant sold eggs for 25¢ a dozen, sauerkraut for 25¢ for three cans, and round steak for 16¢ a pound. Campau Clothing offered genuine Lapaca overcoats for $18.50. At Dave's Radio Sales on Jos. Campau, an automatic washing machine sold for $59. And at Brawer's dime store on Jos. Campau, a little girl's Cinderella frock sold for $1.98. By the 1930s, Jos. Campau, principally between Holbrook and Caniff, had become a premier shopping area anchored by three "dime" stores—Neisner, Grant, and Kresge. There was also a Sears outlet at Jos. Campau and Trowbridge, and numerous other stores, such as Max's Jewelry and Lendzon's. Fine quality clothing became a hallmark of the strip and filled the windows of such stores as Campau Clothing, Witkowski's, Paris Fashions, Jack's Fifth Avenue, Dave Stober's, and Barney's. For some curious reason, the men's shops clustered on the west side of Jos. Campau while the women's shops were on the east side. For the home, there was New York Linoleum & Carpet Company, and for good health, there was Respondek's, which with a marketing strategy that would defy logic today, billed itself as "America's Smallest Drug Store." Western Auto was one of the city's longest-lasting businesses. It offered bicycles, toys, hardware, and other items. A Kroger store opened in May of 1935 on Jos. Campau north of Caniff. It was promoted as the most ultra-modern market in Hamtramck. Decorated in Nile green and silver on the outside, the store featured a refrigerated meat window, electric fish scalers, electric slicers, and vegetable water sprays.

While most of Hamtramck's Jewish population had moved out of the city to northwest Detroit in the 1920s, they maintained ties with Hamtramck through the stores they owned. Virtually anything that someone would want or need was available in the Hamtramck stores, and within easy walking distance. The most convenient way to go shopping was to walk. Even today, one of the attractions of Hamtramck is its easy accessibility.

For recreation, there were plenty of activities besides those provided by the schools. Hamtramck had two bowling alleys, North End Recreation on Jos. Campau near Carpenter, and Playdium, an impressive Greek Revival building on Jos. Campau near Faber in the city's South End. And theaters thrived. Along with a host of mainly Detroit-based Polish acting troupes, the movie houses had a major presence in Hamtramck. By the late 1930s, there were eight theaters in Hamtramck: Oliver, at Oliver and Conant; Martha Washington, at Jos. Campau and Caniff; Farnum on Jos. Campau across from Wyandotte; Pastime, at Jos. Campau near Grayling; Conant, on Conant near Commor; Campau, on Jos. Campau at Edwin; and Star (later named White Star) at Jos. Campau near Hewitt. Most of these theaters didn't last through the onslaught of television in the late 1940s and early 1950s. Farnum survived until 1969, and Martha Washington held on until the early 1980s.

This building is a rare surviving example of a typical corner store, which once were located on almost every other block.

The White Star theater on Jos. Campau in 1939. The theater featured Polish-language movies to appeal to the largely ethnic population. (Courtesy of the Burton Historical Collection, Detroit Public Library.)

The film fare, for the most part, was the same as it was across the nation. The major Detroit theaters, like the Palms and the Fox, received the major Hollywood productions first. The neighborhood theaters got them second, along with a host of newsreels, cartoons, coming attractions, and even occasional live shows, all for just 5¢. Even so, kids would routinely sneak into the theaters through the back doors, which were opened by friends who had bought tickets. Once inside, they would spend a day watching such Saturday fare as *Rhythm in the Clouds*, starring Patricia Elli and Warren Hull, and *A Fight to the Finish* with Don Terry and Rosalind Keith. Forgettable films and forgotten actors, but they made for an entertaining matinee or a way to break the monotony of weekday evenings before the arrival of television. Polish language films also would appear on the bill. In the late 1930s, many Hamtramckans still did not speak English. To attract patrons, the theaters often would offer free dishes with each ticket. These ended up in a lot of kitchens and dining rooms, and some full sets still exist today.

The theaters also provided Hamtramckans an opportunity to see some of their own. John Hodiak was born in 1914 in Hamtramck and was a 1932 graduate of Hamtramck High School, where he had studied dramatics and journalism. After graduation, he worked at WXYZ radio station in Detroit, then went to New York

67

Gail Kobe, a Hamtramck High School graduate, starred in many TV shows in the 1950s and 1960s and had a small part in Cecil B. DeMille's The Ten Commandments.

to gain stage experience. Eventually, he would star on Broadway in *The Caine Mutiny Court Martial*, and appeared in nearly three dozen films, including some major productions. In 1944, he starred in Alfred Hitchcock's classic *Lifeboat*. He also starred in such quality films as *Night into Morning* with Ray Milland, *A Bell for Adano* with Gene Tierney and William Bendix, and *Battleground* with George Murphy and Van Johnson. Hodiak was an established star when he died prematurely in 1955 of a heart attack.

Tom Tyler also died too soon. Born near Albany, New York in 1903, Tyler moved with his parents, Frank and Helen Markowski, to Hamtramck four years later. While working in an area auto plant, Tyler began weightlifting and was noticed by a Hollywood talent scout at a local weightlifting contest. He was soon churning out grade-B Westerns like *Galloping Thur* and *Battling with Buffalo Bill*, as well as dozens of other films. In all, he made 175 films, including starring as the Mummy in the Universal horror film *The Mummy's Hand*. Most notably, he appeared in the classic *The Grapes of Wrath*, and had a pivotal role as Luke Plummer in the John Wayne/John Ford classic *Stagecoach*.

Tyler was also a Saturday matinee favorite with kids as the comic book superhero Captain Marvel. In 1935, he returned to Hamtramck for a New Year's party at St. Anne's Community House where he delighted the kids, sharing milk at lunch. By 1942, he was voted as Hollywood's most successful Western star and was earning $2,000 a week. But by the early 1950s, his health began fading, as did his film career. Plagued with heart problems, he returned to the Hamtramck area to live with his sister. In 1954, at age 50, he died in St. Francis Hospital of heart failure. Like Hodiak, many of Tyler's films are readily available today on videocassette. Over the coming years, Hamtramck would produce other stars and would-be stars. Gail Kobe, another Hamtramck High School graduate, would find great success in the 1950s and 1960s, acting on numerous television shows, including *Perry Mason, Twilight Zone,* and *The Outer Limits.* Peter Similuk never made it big in Hollywood, although he did appear in the film *A Foreign Affair.* And it's worth noting he had a role in the 1950s cult classic *The Hideous Sun Demon.*

Other popular forms of entertainment were the numerous dances held in the parish and club halls around the city. Dances were held for nearly every occasion, such as Valentine's Day, Halloween, and New Year's. Seemingly, every Saturday night there was at least one dance somewhere. Like the movies, they were a cheap form of entertainment. On a more cultural level, the Hamtramck Philharmonic

This is a typical playbill from Farnum Theatre in 1938. Films changed twice a week and, on occasion, a free dinner plate was offered with each ticket.

Orchestra had been formed in 1922 and performed regularly, and amateur acting troupes were organized to perform at the Tau Beta Community House.

Parades were common. The 1927 Centennial Parade, marking the formation of the township, stretched the length of Jos. Campau. Labor Day, Armistice Day, and a host of other reasons prompted parades. And there were many community activities. In 1936, the Chamber of Commerce sponsored a Hamtramck Fall Festival that featured a trip to Hollywood awarded to two girls. The merchants outing at Paris Park in August of 1935 drew 12,000 people.

Through all the challenges of the Great Depression and the years of assimilation into American society, the thread of Polish culture and contact with the Old Country remained strong. The visit by the Polish ambassador to the United States in 1938 saw the city bedecked with red, white, and blue bunting as he spoke at Keyworth Stadium, but he was also entertained by dancing children dressed in traditional and colorful Polish costumes. In May of 1935, the school district marked the death of Polish Marshal Jozef Pilsudski, who twice was leader of Poland and regarded as its "savior," by renaming Playfair Elementary School to Pilsudski School.

Polish dignitaries, authors, and soldiers frequently visited Hamtramck. That was not surprising. By this period, Hamtramck had one of the largest Polish

Gotta dance! All through the Great Depression, dances were held almost every week at such places as the Tau Beta Community House and St. Ladislaus parish, among many others.

populations of any community outside of Poland. The Detroit-based *Dziennik Polski* (*Polish Daily News*) newspaper was reporting on local affairs in Polish by 1908. Hamtramck had its own newspapers, including the *Plain Dealer* and *The Citizen*, among others, which reported the news in English and Polish. *The Citizen* continued with a Polish section until the 1980s when the Polish speaking population declined to a point of making that unnecessary.

With such strong ties to Poland, it wasn't surprising that most of the people of Hamtramck were left stunned and alarmed by the events of September 1, 1939.

Hamtramck loves a parade and, in 1927, thousands turned out along Jos. Campau for the Centennial Jubilee, marking the formation of the third Hamtramck Township in 1827.

4. RETOOLING

In the predawn hours of Thursday, September 1, 1939, the tanks and troops of Nazi Germany rolled across the border into Poland. Facing them was a dedicated but hopelessly undersized Polish army that met the tanks with soldiers on horseback. The fact that the Poles stood up to the Nazis at all and refused Hitler's demands for Polish territory would be a source of pride for Poles for many generations. But pride wouldn't stop a bullet or upend a tank.

The implications, of course, went far beyond Poland, for this was to be a world war. In Hamtramck the impact of the news of the invasion was dramatic. Many Hamtramckans had relatives in Poland and were concerned about their fate. Hamtramckans openly prayed, some on their front lawns. People flooded into churches. Men pored over maps in cafes and clubs to see where the Germans were advancing, and how far that was from their hometowns. Someone hung an effigy of Adolf Hitler from the viaduct on Conant. The initial shock of the news of the invasion was eased somewhat when Great Britain and France entered the war, but that provided scant relief.

But the United States was not at war. This was still a European conflict and, being in a neutral nation, the Poles risked deportation if they attempted to incite the country to war. So, the Poles responded the only way they could—with money. Almost immediately, relief efforts were started for the victims of the war. A campaign to raise $15 million was launched by representatives of 101 Polish fraternal, social, civic, and political organizations that met at St. Stanislaus High School in nearby Detroit the day after the outbreak of the war. "We have already raised $82,000," Chester A Kozdroy, president of the Polish Central Citizen Committee, said at the meeting. Cash-starved Poles gave whatever they could. Over the first weekend of the war, Dad's Delicatessen at Caniff and Jos. Campau reported collecting nearly $10,000 in donations. Some people promised to donate a part of their salaries to the cause.

But the United States was not at war, and many Americans, such as hero Charles Lindbergh, argued against getting involved. They preached isolationism. Let Europe settle its own affairs. Bishop Stephen Woznicki cautioned the Poles not to rattle war sabers. "We must be especially careful that there is no violation in letter or spirit of American neutrality," he urged. The cry around town was

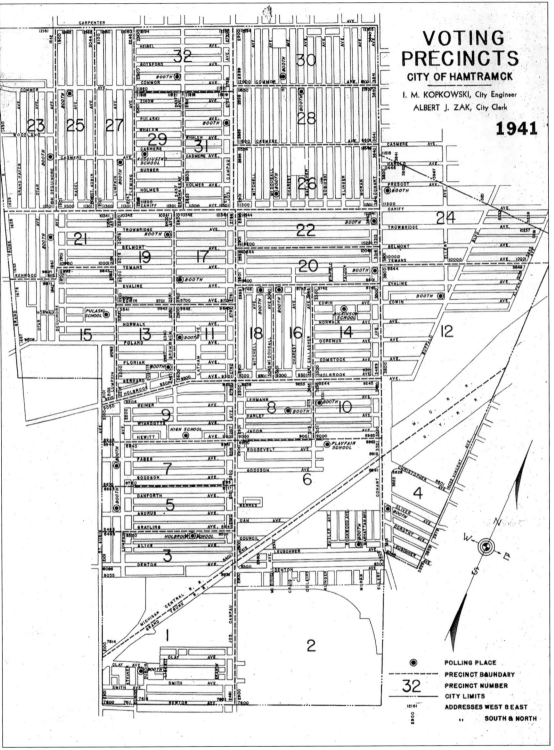

By 1941, Hamtramck had established its familiar borders.

"America first—then Poland." Hamtramck mayor Walter Kanar sympathized with the Poles but called on "all Polish-American organizations in Hamtramck, and all citizens who wish to participate in such expressions of sympathy to cooperate with Bishop Woznicki in whatever may be adopted for this purpose."

But the United States was not at war. The point was hammered over and over again. Despite their strong emotions, most Poles in Hamtramck could do little more than donate money and watch events unfold with horror. The destruction of Poland by the Nazis was especially brutal. Hamtramckan Cecelia Gollon witnessed it first hand. She was studying Polish art, history, and culture at the University of Warsaw when the Germans attacked. She was evacuated from the city during a truce in late September and was able to return to Hamtramck. She brought with her a tale of disaster:

> One half of Warsaw was completely destroyed when I left. The systematic shelling and air bombing by the Germans completely wrecked every building and street in Warsaw. I would say that Warsaw is in complete ruins now and may never be rebuilt to its former grandeur. I was told that many people were killed working in the fields. The Germans would fly low in their planes and machine gun everything and everybody working in the fields. If the Polish army had had more equipment Poland might have held out much longer.

Mayor Rudolph Tenerowicz sits here with a young supporter. (Courtesy of The Citizen.*)*

Such accounts stirred the emotions of the local Poles and led them to contribute more. Over the coming months, a variety of dignitaries trapped outside Poland at the outbreak of the war, as well as others, would come to Hamtramck with their own war stories. Chief among them was General Joseph Haller, described as "one of Poland's greatest living heroes," who spoke to a rally of 3,000 people at Hamtramck High School in February of 1940. He estimated that 300,000 Poles had been killed in the German invasion and pleaded for aid. "Poland fought not only for herself but for democracy and civilization," Haller pleaded. "We ask you now to keep on fighting with us. We need your help and ask that you do all that is possible."

While Europe burned, Hamtramck had continuing problems on the home front, at least in city hall. From its incorporation as a city, Hamtramck's political scene was contentious, to say the least. Bitter political rivalries became typical as alliances were formed and broken. Politics in Hamtramck have always been a personal affair, which to this day colors the picture with shades of animosity. In the 1920s, Prohibition fueled temptation. It already has been noted that the first mayor, Peter C. Jezewski, was convicted for connections to vice operations. He was followed in office in 1926 by Arthur Majewski, who campaigned on a promise to clean up the city. Nevertheless, Majewski ran afoul of the city council that was still loyal to Jezewski, and was not able to do much to stop the stills and close the gambling houses and brothels. In 1928, Majewski's political enemies put forth a new candidate, Dr. Rudolph Tenerowicz, who would prove to be one of the most flamboyant and colorful figures in Hamtramck's history.

Tenerowicz was known and beloved by many Hamtramckans for his services as a doctor. He frequently treated people for free when they could not afford to pay him. He was a handsome man with a ready smile and a good nature. Tenerowicz defeated Majewski and had a relatively uneventful first term as mayor. He was re-elected in 1930 when his opponent, T.T. Dysarz, lost the support of Jezewski, who had resurfaced on the political scene after being released from Leavenworth prison. Not satisfied with their loss, opponents of Tenerowicz launched a recall campaign, which failed. But Tenerowicz had worse things to worry about. In 1932, he, along with two councilmen, the chief of police, a police captain, and the head of a vice racket were indicted by a Wayne County grand jury on charges of collusion with the rackets. The councilmen, supporters of Tenerowicz, were later dropped from the case, but the others, including Tenerowicz, were found guilty and sent to prison for terms of three and a half to five years.

But this melodrama was far from over, and Tenerowicz still had a big role to play. While still indicted, Tenerowicz turned over his office to Jezewski, who was re-elected in 1932. Needless to say, the familiar problems of vice and corruption persisted, and in the convoluted machinations of Hamtramck politics, Joseph Lewandowski surfaced as a new candidate. His supporters skillfully used the Tenerowicz conviction and his ties to Jezewski to win the election of 1934. But Tenerowicz was still in the picture. By 1934, Hamtramck was a solidly Democratic town, and 15,000 citizens signed a petition to free Tenerowicz, which

At the building of the Veterans Memorial park in about 1940 are, from left to right, Anthony Tenerowicz, brother of then-Congressman Dr. Rudolph Tenerowicz; Leroy Smith, of the Wayne County Road Commission; Councilman George Banish; City Engineer I.M. Kopkowski; and Councilmen Ted Zajac and Joe Sawicki.

they presented to Governor William A. Comstock. A Democrat, Comstock noted the solid voting block represented by the petitioners and pardoned Tenerowicz, saying his conviction had been politically motivated. Tenerowicz returned to Hamtramck where he was greeted as if he were a war hero.

The election of 1936 was shaping up to be unlike anything the city had ever seen. Ninety-one candidates were running for 10 offices. The critical race, for mayor, pitted Lewandowski against Tenerowicz. The campaign was especially brutal, with factions of both sides ridiculing each other and playing dirty political tricks, the worst of which was a bomb that blew up next to Lewandowski's garage. In the final count, Tenerowicz defeated Lewandowski by more than 1,000 votes. Two years later, Tenerowicz was elected again despite the fact that his messy divorce made juicy headlines in the local papers. The Tenerowicz story took another turn that year when he ran for, and was elected to, Congress, representing the Hamtramck area. His opponents tried to have him removed from office because of his conviction, but he was too popular with the people, having won the election by a 72,000- to 18,000- vote margin.

Once Tenerowicz resigned as mayor, Councilman Vincent Sadlowski was named acting mayor, but that wasn't the end of the matter. Sadlowski was challenged by Councilman Walter Kanar, who also aspired to be mayor. Because Sadlowski was acting mayor, his vote in the council was challenged by Kanar. The issue was turned over to the state attorney general, who ruled in favor of Kanar. So, in January of 1939, Kanar took over as mayor. The following year he was elected to office by a mere 149 votes over Frank Matulewicz, the city clerk. Kanar was soon embroiled in controversy. Wayne County Circuit Judge Homer Ferguson's one-man grand jury indicted several Hamtramckans on the usual graft charges. More serious, however, was a new set of charges brought against several Hamtramck officials, including Kanar, who was accused of taking a $500 bribe regarding a contract for installing parking meters. Many of the charges were dropped, but Kanar was left in somewhat of a legal limbo. In a tangled set of maneuvers, the governor ordered a hearing be held in probate court regarding the charges against Kanar. Evidence was collected and sent to the governor's office, where it languished. Finally, Kanar brought the matter to an end by resigning in January of 1942.

In later years, Hamtramckans have tended to downplay their early political history. The rampant corruption and convictions were hardly a source of pride: it was history that was better left alone. People have speculated why Hamtramck had such a turbulent past when other cities of a similar size were much more sedate in comparison. Some feel the conflict came as part of the nature of the Polish people. They could be stubborn and proud, and possibly overwhelmed at all that democracy had to offer after decades of oppression at the hands of invaders in their old country. Or possibly, circumstances of time and place may have been to blame.

Prohibition fueled corruption nationwide. There were enormous amounts of money to be made during Prohibition, cooking up gin and beer and operating speakeasies and after-hours clubs. It was common for people to flout the liquor laws, which few lawmakers themselves obeyed, so there was little stigma attached to breaking the laws or even getting caught for breaking them. Everybody did it and almost no one seemed to care. With Hamtramck being so close to Detroit, it was a safe haven for Detroiters, including prominent citizens, who didn't want to risk getting caught in their own city. Hamtramck was delighted to open its doors and bottles to thirsty Detroiters. With such vast amounts of illicit cash flowing, corruption was inevitable. The temptation was too great for many to resist.

In addition, Hamtramck was growing at a phenomenal pace. In the space of 10 years, the area went from a modest village of about 3,000 to a major city of 48,000. Dodge Main poured money into the city with its property taxes. Money was available for many things the growing population needed, as well as for padding payrolls. After all, what difference did it make in the scheme of things if you gave a few friends jobs? And what harm was there in taking a kickback for awarding a city contract? Perhaps little, except when such practices become standard operating procedures. After a while, the system gradually spirals out of control. More people come to the trough and when everybody does it, it doesn't seem so bad. The system feeds on itself, undermining itself and becoming more difficult to change. Eventually something will give. Someone gets too greedy, or the money runs out, and finally the situation becomes too serious to ignore or go unnoticed. That's when grand juries are convened and indictments handed down.

Not all the problems were generated by corruption. Running a city, even in the 1920s and 1930s, was and is a challenging proposition that requires specialized knowledge and skills. Managing budgets, pension systems, payrolls, insurance, federal and state regulations, assessments, tax systems, all these and more, requires a degree of specialized knowledge that city staff too often lacked. Plus, they were under the control of city councils and administrations that had no professional skills in those areas. Running a city is akin to running a business. While a city provides services, not goods and not at a profit, it has to have good financial practices. Too often, Hamtramck has not.

Further, Hamtramck traditionally has been challenged by its own appreciation of democracy. Politics have always been a rough game in town. In the Depression years, it was not unusual for dozens of political meetings to be held nightly during election seasons. Even today, Hamtramckans take their politics very seriously. That's a two-edged sword. It's hard to criticize someone for being civically responsible, but too often that dedication blinds reason. What should be minor differences become impenetrable walls because they turn personal. The kind of bickering and sniping that has plagued Hamtramck politics over the decades occurs in other cities too. Even upscale communities, where city councils and administrations are filled with lawyers and business executives, are not immune. It's part of human nature.

Dodge Main continued to grow over the years, reaching an eight-story height by 1930.

Even in its earliest years, Copernicus Junior High School had such amenities as this student broadcasting studio.

Whatever the reasons for the political raucousness, Hamtramck has continued to survive and thrive. Even in spite of itself. For whatever was going on in city hall, life outside went on at a sure pace.

Such was the situation in early December of 1941. Mayor Walter Kanar was under a cloud of controversy as the bribery charges were pending. Other events occupied the residents as well. The war in Europe lumbered on. The Knights of Columbus Council Number 2723 voted to buy a U.S. Defense Bond of at least $100 every two months. The city council was considering acquiring land on Holbrook to use for a YMCA site. The kids at Copernicus Junior High School were getting ready to go on the air with a special program on WJBK radio. Eight gyms and two indoor swimming pools were set to open in a few days to kick off the winter recreation program. Christmas decorations were going up and people were shopping, although money was still tight. But George the Drummer ("Wind him up and he beats the drum") sold for 29¢ at Brawer's, and a Max Factor special makeup set ("Secrets of Lovely Beauty in a Gay Holiday Box—Face Powder, Rouge, Tru-color Lipstick, Cleansing Cream, and Brillox") made a great Christmas gift for only $3.95 at Respondek's Original Cut Rate Drugs. Max's Jewelry intoned that it "Now makes possible the Christmas gift that will really be appreciated—Give them glasses—the sensible Christmas gift." That's eye, not drinking. But don't party too hearty. Ten thousand posters warning that over-indulgers get "90 days for drunk driving" had been placed throughout the metro Detroit area.

Sunday, December 7, 1941. Pearl Harbor was attacked and the United States was suddenly at war.

Tuesday, December 9, 1941. Volunteers for Hamtramck's civil defense program began reporting to the public schools, although what need they could fill was debatable. Hamtramck was thousands of miles from the war in Europe and many thousands of miles more from Pearl Harbor in Hawaii. Nevertheless, Hamtramck would be prepared . . . for whatever.

Mayor Kanar appointed William B. Perske, Stephen Wrobel Jr., and Stephen Matron to the Civil Defense Council. The Common Council appointed George A. Banish to represent it on the Defense Council, and the council almost immediately requested $500,000 from Governor Murray D. Van Waggoner to prepare for any emergency. The money would be used to buy police, fire, and hospital supplies. City Engineer I.M. Kopkowski suggested that a $100,000 bond proposal be presented to the voters.

By the end of the war, the Civil Defense patrol members were being taught to deal with bomb-carrying balloons sent aloft by the Japanese. The Civil Defense director warned that the Japanese had planned to put suicide pilots on the balloons. In any case, residents were advised not to approach or touch "any object resembling a bomb-carrying balloon." And any person who found such a balloon was told to report it to the nearest Civil Defense official or the police. However, no balloon bombs made it to Hamtramck, although a few did land on the West Coast.

On a more immediate and realistic level, the Red Cross stationed a mobile unit at the Tau Beta Community House to collect blood donations. Within a matter of weeks, the Red Cross also collected more than $9,000 in donations for the war effort. City volunteers also began going door to door to collect enough money to pay for a bomber "to scrap the Japs." The draft had already been instituted, and local men began joining the armed forces.

Acting Mayor Anthony Tenerowicz (Rudolph's brother), who replaced Kanar upon his resignation in January 1942, made a radio appeal to all Hamtramckans to turn in shovels, picks, drums, hammers, axes, rubber rain coats, and any other objects that could be used for the war effort. "This drive, the first of its kind in the country, is being undertaken to secure urgently needed Civilian Defense supplies and also to relieve the burden on manufacturers. If Hamtramck is successful in this drive, we will become the leaders for the entire nation."

Newly designated Civil Defense wardens again went door to door, this time advising people on how to prepare for an emergency, including clearing the houses entirely of all unnecessary articles, which would make a fire worse in an air raid. Residents were also advised to have a flashlight for every person in the house; to keep handy bags of sand, a small first aid kit, a shovel, dark eyeglasses, and bucket; and to put material over the windows to black them out. For an emergency, each house should have a "refuge room," in which there should be no or few windows, a supply of water, reading material, a toilet, a portable radio, and a sturdy table.

In retrospect, this all may seem rather quaint today, but it was a very serious matter in the wake of the attack on Pearl Harbor. In fact, no one knew exactly what to expect. While it didn't seem likely the Japanese were going to land on the beaches of Belle Isle, the threat of enemy infiltration and sabotage were quite real. Detroit was an industrial powerhouse that was quickly being converted into a war machine. By the spring, the draft and industry gearing up for the war effort were beginning to have an effect on the unemployment rate. For the week ending March 28, 1942, Hamtramck workers filed 3,068 claims for unemployment insurance; that was a decline of 264 claims from the previous week. "The crying need is for skilled tool-room workers to help the changeover of civilian plants to war production work," said James R. Lyon, manager of the U.S. Employment Service office.

Prior to the attack, American industry had been boosted somewhat with efforts to supply the British, but with the Pearl Harbor attack, full attention was given to converting civilian production to the war effort. By February 1942, civilian auto production was ended and full military production began. Chrysler built a new plant in Warren to turn out tanks. Ford built a new plant in Ypsilanti to produce B-24 bombers. As 600,000 men and women went into the armed forces, there was

With the outbreak of World War II, a Civil Defense system was organized by Hamtramck. This continued through the 1950s, with the advent of the Cold War. Here, Mayor Albert Zak and Councilman Martin Dulapa look over a new rescue truck.

a severe need for new workers. Finally, jobs were plentiful. The Great Depression was over.

But at what price? Nearly every household was affected as someone in the family went into the service. A large marker was placed in front of city hall, listing every Hamtramckan who went into the service. People began to take new interests in atlases to locate exotic places like New Caledonia, Wake Island, and Iwo Jima. And so it went for four years. Bond drives were held. On August 17, 1942, comedians Bud Abbott and Lou Costello performed at Keyworth Stadium for everyone who bought at least $1 in war bonds. A victory bond drive led to the payment of a B-17 bomber named *The City of Hamtramck*, which took part in raids over Germany. Blackouts were staged to test the Civil Defense system, and collection of material for the war continued. Gas rationing began in September of 1942, and soon ration books became a familiar sight. Stella Zadroga stopped by city hall and was congratulated by new Mayor Stephen Skrzycki. She was Hamtramck's first WAAC, or member of the Women's Army Auxiliary Corps.

Inevitably, the notifications of casualties started to arrive. Marine Corporal John Targosz Jr. was the first Hamtramckan killed in action in October 1942, in the Solomon Islands in the Pacific. The family was stunned at the news, but his father was proud of his son, "who loved to fight and loved his country." Ultimately, 194 Hamtramckans would die in the war.

In war, life settled into a new routine. But what was it really like? The best way to see the picture is through the eyes of one who lived the experience. Former Hamtramckan Irene Namiotka Jordan remembered it this way:

> I attended St. Florian, a Catholic Polish school taught by the good Felician sisters. I remember that when I was bad and the nun sent a note home to my parents with me, I delivered it. I never read it. I delivered it. I also remember that generally resulted in a talking to and being strapped for driving a nun, or as my mother referred to it, "a holy person" to the point of exasperation. I remember getting rapped across the knuckles for hesitating and halting during my recitation of the Polish alphabet. But to this day I can recite it by heart.
>
> I remember cutting out hundreds of little camels off Camel cigarette packages to do bulletin boards during Christmas throughout the whole school, it seemed. Don't ask me where the nun got that many packages, but it was during the war and we used to collect scrap and tinfoil from cigarettes. I don't know what the war effort did with it, but I remember doing that. I can only assume the nun had every father smoking Camels and collecting the tinfoil for the war effort and the camel pictures for me so I could help her with those boards.
>
> I remember we were taken out twice a day for what I call an airing. You know how lazy the mind gets after a couple of hours of lecturing and reciting. Well, just about the time you thought you'd actually fall asleep, out they would take you. We would go around a square block

The Forensics Club at Hamtramck High School struck a formal pose in June 1946.

area, down Florian, up Latham, along Poland and back down Brombach and back into the school. In those days there were no school lunches. This was a private school, so you walked home to eat and back again. There were no Christmas, Easter week breaks, no teacher breaks. There were no field trips or outings.

Christmases were really nice around our house. You did not ask for much and you knew not to expect too much. But you believed in Santa Claus. We knew we could not expect a doll, for example, but we did not realize we were poor because every other kid on the block was in the same position, especially if he came from a big family. I remember it was amazing what my grandmother could do with two oranges. She would cut them into quarters and eighths and we would each get two pieces with our oatmeal, and that would be breakfast. And maybe there would be corn meal bread piping hot out of the stove each morning. I remember that stove. It was a wood burner and stood in the kitchen as a point of central heat for the kitchen and one bedroom. We used to polish it with grease from a can on Saturday to keep it shiny, and as the newspaper was dipped into the grease and then swished on top the stove it would begin to fry and fill the kitchen with a sort of greasy but real homey smell.

Saturdays were cleaning days and we each had a task to do. We lived in a typical two-by-two house. In other words, there were two living

The Blue and Gold Star Mothers march down Jos. Campau on Memorial Day, 1955 on their way to laying a wreath at the veterans' monument at Veterans Memorial Park. Following World War II, numerous veterans and support groups were formed.

quarters in one house. Most were up and down (with families living on upper and lower flats). Ours was front and back. My uncle lived in front in the four rooms with his wife and child. We lived in back with dad and mom and the rest of the kids. We slept three in a bed and the place was heated by a big pot-belly stove in the sitting room, which was fed coal.

In those days, you worked at whatever you could find. Dad was a garbage man. He was a dog catcher. He was a night watchman. But I do remember that when he came through the door, no matter how he smelled, we hung onto him because he was daddy and he was home. I was surprised later in life as I traced my family roots to find he was mere five-foot-eight on his declaration of citizenship papers. To me, he was a giant.

As winter melted into spring, we looked forward to May. May was special. We had this church thing going. Almost the whole city got involved. I mean, what could you expect, being Polish. Catholic. Three churches all doing the same thing within walking distance of one another. The first of May was considered May Day. We had a senior from high school, who had good grades, attendance at Mass and took Communion daily be the one who would crown the statue being carried by the Knights of Columbus. The church bells would ring at 10 a.m. and no matter what you were doing, you generally ran down the corner to Latham and Brombach to watch the procession. There would be the

Girls Sodality, the Ladies Altar Guild, the Holy Name Society, the Blue and Gold Star Mothers, the Knights of Columbus and choirs and, last of all, the statue of the Virgin Mary with a group of priests with the pastor under the canopy blessing us as he went along the route. It was something grand to see. People kneeling down and crossing themselves under the heavenly blue sky. That lasted about one hour and ended with the crowning of the statue with a wreath of flowers.

Summers were very eventful. There was a guy next door who, in a day when such things were unheard of, wanted to be a miniature race car driver. We all thought he was nuts. He tinkered with that car, and *va-va-vroom* could be heard all over the neighborhood. His mother was a dear friend of my mother, and we always thought her a rather strange lady. To us (age 7 or 8) she looked 80, with pitch black hair that she wore in a bun around the nape of her neck. When she unrolled it to comb it it reached below her waist. In those days of no doctors, she was the midwife, the doctor. She dispensed a medical knowledge to the local mothers, based on years of experience, and whispered secret formulas from the Old Country.

Images of those days linger, ingrained in one's soul. Images like an eight-hour school day . . . the dances in which the nuns would measure the distance between you and your partner as you danced . . . the daily Masses . . . the punishment for wearing too much makeup . . . "The Lone Ranger" on the radio . . . dates on the front porch where you talked and ate ice cream and cake that mom offered . . . six friends piling into a

It's Government Affairs Day for students of St. Ladislaus High School in 1948 as they visit the city offices on Jos. Campau.

car and going to Belle Isle to rent a canoe . . . the Baker Streetcar . . . Farnum sweetshop, Leo Miller Funeral Home . . . Hamtramck High . . . Cunningham's Drug store, the dress shops . . . the linen shops . . . Federal's, where most of us shopped . . . Lendzon's—with its wooden floor . . . Podezwa's Shoes, which catered to the nun and priest trade . . . Wonder Bazaar, which sold all the religious things you needed for First Communion . . . Harry the Hatter . . . the paint store owned by the Feldmans and run by their in-laws, the Goodmans, who I was babysitter for at age 14 . . . Dr. Bell, the black dentist that everyone went to . . . the wading pool at Holbrook and Conant . . . tennis at the park . . . Fourth of July fireworks at Keyworth Stadium . . . sitting on the front porch and talking to the people who walked by . . . going to the store to buy two carrots and a celery stalk and asking for a soup bone for free . . . milk delivered in glass bottles to your door . . . looking at the leeches at P.C. Jezewski's drug store . . . the sing-song cry of 'tomatoes-potatoes-get-your-onions-fresh' from the back of a truck . . . making margarine with lard and a package of orange powder . . . adding chicory to the coffee to make it last longer . . . Polish bands like Johnny Sadrack . . . a double feature at Campau theater . . . mother curling her hair using strips of white sheet she had torn into pieces . . . the guy who worked nights yelling at the kids to go play in the alley . . . Ziegfeld cutout dolls . . . what seemed like long journeys to Warren and Sterling Heights . . . collecting scrap metal, tinfoil and grease for the war effort . . . and relishing bacon drippings on black bread. . . .

It was a glorious experience of family ties, love, respect, civic duty, pride, ignorance, new vision, and I would not trade places with the woman of today for a million bucks.

In the pre-rock 'n' roll era, this was a hot act at Hamtramck High School.

The American flag flies over Zussman Park, named after Medal of Honor winner Lt. Raymond Zussman. At right is City Hall.

Life was quite different across the sea. Soldiers and civilians were still dying. The death of each soldier was a tragedy, but most passed without much notice except to the families affected. One Hamtramckan especially stood out, however. Lieutenant Raymond Zussman was 27 years old in September of 1944 when he was moving forward with the United States troops through France after the landing at Normandy. He was in command of two tanks operating with an infantry company near Noroy Le Bourg, France. One tank became bogged down and Zussman decided to push ahead with the other tank. They soon ran into a roadblock, which Zussman ordered the tank to destroy. At once, German soldiers in hiding opened fire. Zussman stood his ground, exposed to gunfire at the side of the tank as bullets bounced off the metal around him. He returned fire and in moments, three of the Germans were dead and eight others surrendered. More gunfire came at the G.I.s and Zussman pointed out and directed fire at a German vehicle nearby. Three more Germans were killed, and more than a half-dozen surrendered, but Zussman wasn't done. He led the tank into the town, where they encountered more heavy fire. Zussman directed the tank to return fire, and in minutes, another 20 Germans surrendered. Zussman again went ahead and again drew enemy fire, this time in the form of thrown hand grenades, but Zussman eluded the blasts and directed the tank to the Germans. It fired through the back door of a building and 11 more Germans surrendered.

Zussman pressed ahead into the center of town. The tank crew lost sight of him, but there soon came the sound of a Tommy gun. A few minutes later, a stream of German prisoners began rounding the corner of a building, 30 in all,

Following the end of World War II, civilian production resumed at Dodge Main.

followed by Zussman and his Tommy gun. Later that day, Zussman captured a truck and its driver. Zussman had almost single-handedly liberated the town of Noroy Le Bourg. Within days, Zussman was recommended for a Congressional Medal of Honor. He would receive it posthumously. Several days after his heroism at Noroy Le Bourg, Zussman was killed in action.

Later, the Zussman family would donate a square piece of property in front of St. Francis Hospital to be used as a neighborhood park. This one-square block of land, ever since called Zussman Park, is crossed by concrete walks that converge at a circular area, 27 feet in diameter, at the center of the park. There is a flagpole at the site now, but until World War II, a large cannon from World War I stood solidly there. Children used to play on it and people would pose for pictures by it until it was melted down to be used for the second great war effort, which cost Lieutenant Zussman his life. The park became his memorial. For most others, the only testimonial to their sacrifice was a brief mention in the newspaper. About the time that Lieutenant Zussman was earning his Medal of Honor, the local papers were listing the lost soldiers.

Lieutenant Albert Kukorowski, son of Mr. and Mrs. Carl Kukorowski of Moran Street, was killed in action on July 6. He was a B-17 bombardier-navigator and had participated in the Tunisian, Sicilian, and Italian campaigns during eight months in service overseas. Private First Class Chester Romanowski was killed in France on July 9. He was the son of Mr. and Mrs. Joseph Romanowski of Casmere Street. Richard Ellsworth Hiller was a gunner's mate, third class in the navy. Many more were wounded.

The agony ended on August 14, 1945, when the news of Japan's surrender was announced by President Harry Truman at 7:00 p.m. An estimated 25,000 people poured onto Jos. Campau and Caniff to create the local version of Times Square in what was called the greatest celebration in the city's history. Cars jammed the length of Jos. Campau as people blew their horns, throwing confetti and streamers. As many as 15 teenagers waving flags and shouting piled into one car that rolled along Jos. Campau. The American Legion staged an impromptu parade, carrying flags down Jos. Campau. All the stores closed and many hung flags on their windows to discourage revelers from damaging them. A car dragged an effigy of Emperor Hirohito behind it. Women kissed soldiers and sailors in the street. The clamor lasted until 1:00 a.m., and the police just stepped aside, letting the celebrating go on unhampered. Police Chief Joseph Trojnarski reported that not a single window had been broken. Many stores and businesses, including Dodge Main, stayed closed the following day.

It was finally over. Soon husbands, sons, and daughters would be coming home. Some, who had been drafted in the months before the attack on Pearl Harbor, had been gone for nearly five years. Leaves home were sporadic, but often productive. Baby Boomers began arriving even before the war had ended, but some toddlers were faced with adjusting to a father they had never even seen.

More difficult, however, was the return to civilian jobs—or lack of them. Towards the end of the war, when war materiel production slowed, the dreaded unemployment lines began to swell again. Within weeks of the end of the war, thousands of workers were laid off. So many people were filing for unemployment that the Michigan Unemployment Compensation Commission opened a second office in the Ukrainian Hall on Carpenter just to handle the new claims. Lines of people filing for unemployment grew to huge proportions. People brought chairs to sit on while waiting in the August sun. And thousands were added to the lines daily as companies faced cancellation of contracts due to the end of the war. The Manpower Commission and Unemployment Commission both ominously reported that unemployment in the Hamtramck-North Detroit area hit 300,000.

Nevertheless, the fears of a new Depression would not be realized. Despite the rising unemployment, the cycle of supply and demand kicked in, and people had a supply of money saved up during the war years when there were no large items to buy. During the war, production boomed at Dodge Main, swelling the work force to 40,000. Almost all civilian auto production had been halted during the war, so that meant no car was newer than four years old in 1945. The returning soldiers were a lot more worldly when they returned home, and they wanted cars.

Auto companies returned to civilian production and began rolling out the iron. Smaller old companies were revived and new car companies were founded. Studebaker, Nash, Willys, Crosley, Hudson, and Kaiser-Frazer fought for market share with the major producers, General Motors, Ford, and Chrysler. These would be short-lived, however, as they were swallowed up by the Big Three in the next decade. Only Hudson and Nash would survive by merging to become American Motors. The Big Three had the resources that the smaller companies couldn't match by being able to switch back to civilian production. And at Dodge Main, production was greater than ever. Another factor that contributed to the strength of the post-war economy was that the United States industrial infrastructure was intact, unlike in Europe and Asia, where they had suffered heavy wartime damage. American factories were functioning and able to produce what the world market wanted.

With the war over, attention started turning back to domestic matters. Of course, throughout the early war years, Hamtramck continued to evolve in ways that had nothing to do with the war. Just beating the imposition of war rationing and war shortages, the city's Ukrainian community managed to complete Immaculate Conception Ukrainian Catholic Church on the city's north side in 1941. A magnificent structure, it was patterned after the Hagia Sophia in Istanbul. In 1942, the city, with the federal government, constructed the Colonel Hamtramck Homes, a housing project at the northwest corner of the city. Its intent was to provide low-cost housing to needy persons. From its beginning, however, it became embroiled in controversy as the Housing Commission tried to keep African Americans out of the units. Ultimately, the courts ruled that the housing project had to be integrated, but not before more than 10 years of litigation.

The schools also had their share of controversy, leading up to a charge that four school board members had accepted bribes to sell jobs. Without the steady and nearly unchallenged hand of Superintendent Keyworth, the school system lost much of its direction, although the schools continued to offer their innovative programs and services.

Immaculate Conception Ukrainian Catholic Church was constructed in 1941, just before the outbreak of World War II.

Mayor Stephen Skrzycki would share a musical moment. (Courtesy of The Citizen.)

Charges of corruption, calls for grand jury investigation, and political squabbling continued unabated in the 1940s. Every so often, the police would still uncover a bathtub gin operation in some house, but none of that amounted to much. No more mayors were sent to prison. The political scene remained lively. In 1942, Dr. Stephen Skrzycki was elected mayor and almost immediately came under fire for being a "part-time" mayor, dividing his time between city hall and his medical practice. Skrzycki also incurred the wrath of the labor unions for trying to fire 90 union employees and for opposing the adoption of Civil Service. Even so, Skrzycki was reelected and held office until 1952.

In the late 1940s, Hamtramck was still a Democratic stronghold. The national election of 1948 reinforced the point. Democrat Harry Truman lambasted Republican Thomas Dewey 15,317 votes to 2,249 votes. Nothing new there.

Politics aside, things were changing in many ways. The United States went into World War II in biplanes and came out four years later on the blast of two nuclear bombs. Jet planes soon were common in the military and not far away from civilian use. The sound barrier was cracked, and the days of the ice box were fading fast. Car sales were booming and people were becoming more willing to pay steep prices for those new contraptions called televisions.

At first, stores would place TVs in their windows where they would quickly attract clusters of viewers. Bars also brought in sets where patrons got their first taste of the programming, as limited as it was. Al Ziskie's Bar on Jos. Campau pulled in customers with "the largest screen in the city—4-foot-by 6-foot." Soon people were buying sets of their own. In 1949, Tondry's Home Appliance Shop on Jos. Campau offered a fine console with a screen of about 8 by 8 inches, with an AM-FM Victrola radio-phonograph, for a whopping $550 (installation extra).

BOWERY NITE CLUB

12050 Jos. Campau   Hamtramck, Mich.

YOUR HOST

FRANK BARBARO

Stick with him to the Finish- Buy More Bonds

"KNOWN FROM COAST TO COAST"

CHOICE FOODS ～～～ FINE LIQUORS

Frank Barbaro's Bowery Nite Club was already well-known in 1944 when this photo holder was printed, urging patrons to "Stick with him to the finish—Buy more Bonds." Patrons who had their photos taken at the Bowery would receive this complimentary holder.

But you could take up to 65 weeks to pay. Compare that cost to $189 for a refrigerator and $89 for a sewing machine.

As the decade came to a close, conditions in the city were verging on boring. The headlines told the stories. In March, the city got a second-place trophy for winning a clean-up project. Francis Koltuniak won a $10 first-place prize in a crossword puzzle contest sponsored by area merchants and the *Plain Dealer* newspaper. Seven Hamtramck school teachers won awards for 15 consecutive years of Catholic instruction. More significantly, opponents of Walter Reuther won control of Dodge Local 3 in UAW-CIO elections held in March. Local 3 was one of the key UAW union locals, tracing its past to the 1937 sit-down strike, which by this time seemed ancient history. The late 1940s also produced a major campaign to stamp out tuberculosis. A mobile unit was parked at the Tau Beta Community House and at Dodge Local 3 on Jos. Campau to administer chest X-rays. By the time the campaign ended in April of 1949, more than 10,000 people had had X-rays. At that time, tuberculosis and polio were still serious health threats.

Despite that, this was an era of good times, and people wanted to have fun. Johnny Sadrack, "The National Polka King," was a top area entertainer and could be found playing at most of the area clubs. In fact, there were plenty of bands and venues. Henry Kolodziejczyk and his Cavaliers provided lively dancing music. Not everybody liked polkas, so you might hear the somewhat incongruous Alphonse Bonavia at the piano at Bienkowski's Bar on Conant, and Joey Scott and his accordion was "on the spot" at the venerable House of Rau. But of all the clubs, none had the prestige of The Bowery. That club on Jos. Campau was known across the Midwest and attracted some of the top entertainers in the country.

Through the 1940s and into the early 1950s, The Bowery nurtured a growing reputation as a top-rated night club. Owner Frank Barbaro promoted the club as the place to see "Your favorite radio and movie stars, direct from Hollywood." It was not an exaggeration. Jimmy Durante, the Three Stooges, Johnny Desmond, Gypsy Rose Lee, Milton Berle, Sally Rand, Tony Martin, the Harmonicats, Ella Fitzgerald, Joe E. Lewis, Helen Morgan, and Sophie Tucker performed there. And occasionally a star would sneak out the back into the alley and go a few doors down to what is now Jean's bar where they could have a quiet drink.

The Barbaros' divorce in the early 1950s left The Bowery in the hands of Mrs. Barbaro and it closed soon afterwards. The building was bought by another of Hamtramck's great businessmen, Woodrow W. Woody of Woody Pontiac. Eventually, The Bowery was demolished and now is a parking lot.

It wasn't the only loss Hamtramck would soon experience.

The Delta Rhythm Boys were headliners at the "air-cooled" Bowery night club in 1945.

5. IN REVERSE

Too many people, too little space.

In the 1930s, when Hamtramck's population topped 56,000 in its 2.1-square-mile area, people were packed in like cars in a used car lot. But there were almost no cars. Few people could afford them, so there was not a great demand for parking spaces. Most houses were built on 30-foot lots, which left little if any room for garages. No matter. Just about any place in Hamtramck was easily within walking distance. Kids walked to school. Moms walked to the corner store, which was located on just about every second corner. For large items or to do some real shopping, folks walked to Jos. Campau. Even today, one can live quite comfortably in Hamtramck without a car. Banks, stores, churches, video stores, drug stores, grocery stores, the library, and city hall are all a relatively easy walk from anywhere in town.

Living was not always comfortable. As many as four families might occupy one house. Each family would get three rooms, two sets upstairs and two downstairs. It was livable, but left little space for such amenities as closets. Still, most people didn't have many clothes in the early days, so the demand for closets wasn't great. Although builders rushed to throw up as many houses on a street as they could as fast as they could, a surprisingly diverse range of house styles appeared.

The overwhelmingly favored style was the traditional front-gable National design. This basic rectangle allowed the house to extend deeply into the narrow lot, but a fair number of Colonials, brick and frame, were also built. Examples of quaint Queen Annes, with their shingled walls, and elegant Tudors can still be found. Even a few Craftsman homes were built, characterized by low, wide-eaved roofs with decorative, exposed beams and columns that often extended to the ground. These were made popular in the 1890s and early 1900s by two California designers. Some were sold as kits that could be bought through a catalog, such as Sears, and were available for less than $2,000. They were assembled on site.

A few unique homes were built around the same time period, including an unusual pyramid-style house, built as a simple square with a roof that extended up from all four sides. Another eye-catcher was a superb Federalist building next to Our Lady Queen of Apostles Church. Many houses were built from the same floor plans, so it's possible to find mirror copies of houses around the city.

Traditionally, Hamtramck's premiere block of homes has been a set of classic brick Georgian and Colonial Revivals on Gallagher between Casmere and Commor. Over the years, this area has been referred to (with a smile) as "Hamtramck Heights."

In fact, Hamtramck was built as a working-class town, despite some homes that clearly belonged to the bosses. And as fine as many were, in the post–World War II years, they were just not adequate for the growing families of Baby Boomers. The whole metro Detroit area was expanding outward as Detroit laid out the infrastructure for its own near-demise. Freeways were built through the neighborhoods, slashing communities and separating people from their churches, but offering them an open road to the suburbs. And they made commuting possible, even over long distances. Detroit built water and sewer lines that linked the suburbs into one huge network of service. While this gave Detroit control of the system, it also made the suburbs even more inviting. Farmland that relied on well water was being converted to subdivisions with all the amenities of the city and with vastly more room. People who could afford to have two cars in Hamtramck, but had no place to park them, could have a garage for as many cars as they could buy. Resident parking became so bad that in May of 1950, more than 100 persons swamped the city council meeting to complain that employees of the nearby General Motors Chevrolet Gear and Axle plant were taking all of their spaces.

The suburbs also had the attraction of wide lawns, both in front and in back. You could buy a house with a lawn measured in acres. In Hamtramck, residents might have a few hundred square feet of space for grass and maybe a few tiny garden plots. In the Depression, people weren't concerned much with lawns, but with the sophistication and affluence of the post-war years, the lure of the suburbs

There are several classic Craftsman-style houses around Hamtramck.

grew stronger. The most popular destination was Warren, just a few miles north of Hamtramck. The even wider-open spaces of Sterling Heights beckoned beyond. Fire was another issue of concern. Most homes in Hamtramck were made of wood, and being so close together, any home fire could prove disastrous, as flames would quickly jump from house to house. Hamtramck firefighters became experts at quickly isolating and containing fires. In the suburbs, however, fire posed less of a threat, as most homes were being made of brick.

Hamtramck's population decline actually began within a few years of its peak. In 1940, the population stood at 48,838. Ten years later, the number was down to 43,355. These figures were not alarming: rather, they were a natural leveling off of the population to a more manageable number. Poles still made up the overwhelming majority of residents: 81 percent in 1940 and 75 percent in 1950. Nevertheless, the downward population trend was established.

In June of 1950, the school board decided to close Marshal Pilsudski School. District enrollment had declined to less than 4,000 students, and the building would no longer be needed. That wasn't the end of the structure, which had been erected in 1921 on the old Stocker farmland: it was destined to become the new city municipal offices. The old city offices, on Jos. Campau, were becoming hazardous. Three chunks of concrete fell off the building façade at one point. No one was injured, but it encouraged the city to seek new quarters.

While the population was on a downward trend, in many other ways, Hamtramck was growing. Just three weeks into the new decade of the 1950s, the

The kids at Pulaski School staged their own parade in 1958.

The American Legion Bushway Post and bugler William Frederyck in February 1947.

dedication of the Polish American Century Club on Holbrook was held. Covering 6,000 square feet, the building was hailed as the city's "most modern club building." Later in 1950, the Polish Falcons Nest 86 opened a $140,000 building at Klinger and Caniff. Our Lady Queen of Apostles parish began constructing a new church on Conant, while Immaculate Conception Ukrainian Catholic parish began building a $350,000 school building. The Polish National Alliance closed out the year by dedicating a new $128,750 hall on Conant.

Although Hamtramck would host a variety of social organizations, such as the Rotary, Lions, and Kiwanis, and many Polish-based social organizations over the years, the end of World War II spurred the creation of numerous veterans' organizations. The membership of these grew even more with the Korean War, which had far less impact on Hamtramck. Economically, the new round of war production lifted employment at Dodge Main, which had fallen after World War II, back up to about 33,000 workers. While hundreds of families were touched by the tragedy of a lost loved one in World War II, Hamtramck suffered 16 casualties in the Korean War. The city had a huge veteran population, and in 1952, plans were made to erect a stately, gray, stone monument at Veterans Memorial Park on the city's South End. Every name of the city's war casualties was engraved on the monument. In the next decade, more would be added for those who would die in Vietnam.

On the political scene, the year 1952 was also especially significant. Mayor Skrzycki was facing a strong challenge from Albert Zak, a state representative and

Mayor Stephen Skrzycki (front row, second from left) goes over documents with city officials around 1950. To Skrzycki's left is then city clerk Albert Zak, who would go on to defeat Skrzycki and become mayor.

former city clerk. The campaign was unusually rough. After 10 years in office, Skrzycki was in trouble. He had run afoul of the city union for trying to lay off union employees and trailed Zak by 1,086 votes in the primary election. Skrzycki campaigned on the platform that he had been untouched by scandal during his tenure, had paid off $4 million in city debt and had placed the city in an excellent financial position. Zak billed himself as "the man with the plan for Hamtramck," promising better recreation and health programs, slum clearance, and more jobs.

Anthony Tenerowicz was a significant name on the primary ballot, since he had briefly filled in as mayor when Walter Kanar resigned in 1942. Also, Walter Gajewski, who had been elected city clerk in 1950 and would serve for nearly 30 years in office, making him one of the longest serving politicians in America, found his name on the ballot. William V. Kozerski made an unsuccessful bid for council, but he would rise later to become mayor. Joseph Lewandowski, the former mayor, would easily be elected as justice of the peace. In the general election held in April, Zak triumphed, soundly defeating Skrzycki, 7,951 to 6,660 votes. Heading the list of council candidates was Julia Rooks, who became only the second councilwoman and first female council president, in Hamtramck's history. (Mary Zuk preceded her.) Rooks, known for her trademark hats, would remain a well respected city official during her nearly 18 years of service.

The spotlight was on Zak. He was the first real politician to be elected as mayor. Politics and public service would remain the core of his life literally to the moment of his death, which occurred in 1975 at the parking lot of the Clock restaurant where he had gone just after leaving a city council meeting.

On the stage of Copernicus Junior High School, on the evening of April 15, 1952, Zak's vision of the future was focused on the city as he made his inaugural address. And he did not like what he saw. He told more than 800 persons attending that he was calling for a full accounting of the city's finances. "My first goal is to obtain $363,285 to run the city without increasing taxes." He claimed that figure to be the amount of the projected budget shortfall. Zak also promised that the city's streets and alleys would be cleaned. It was a promise he would keep, and during his tenure, all the alleys were paved with asphalt and street sweepers were constantly on the move. Whatever the perceptions of the city's financial conditions, plans were being laid for its future development.

In June of 1952, Zak submitted a proposal to the city council to clear slum areas. Zak and city attorney Chester Pierce met with Arthur Shelton of the federal Housing and Home Finance Agency to discuss the possibility of getting grants for urban renewal. The federal government had been giving a heightened priority to urban renewal across the country through the Housing Act of 1949. Hamtramck needed the aid. The census of 1950 showed that of the city's 12,500 housing units,

City Councilwoman Julia Rooks donates to the Disabled Americans Veterans Auxiliary during a regular fund drive in the 1950s.

1,886 failed to meet "normal" housing standards. And 64 still did not have toilets. Under the terms of the Housing Act, all projects had to be local and initiated, approved, and carried out by the community, with a portion of the cost paid by the community. The federal government monitored the programs only to confirm that they were being carried out in accordance with the Act. This would have grave significance for the city in the decade to come.

Ultimately, the program that would be adopted would focus primarily on the city's South End. This area of Hamtramck, south of Holbrook, was the oldest section of town. Hamtramck grew northward over the years from its southern border. The housing stock there was the oldest in town, as were the buildings on Jos. Campau, which date back to 1913 and are still standing. For reasons that have never been clear, the South End has always been a somewhat neglected part of the city. Clay Street, across from Dodge Main, and the Wyandotte-Geimer-Hewitt area just south of Holbrook, were identified as primary areas needing renewal. A series of dilapidated "flat top" multi-family housing units on Wyandotte were definite targets of removal, in addition to a smaller apartment building site on Goodson Street. While the program began innocently and with good intentions, it would evolve into a nightmarish situation in the late 1960s.

But in the 1950s, no one had any concept that the seeds for disaster were taking root. Mayor Zak was focusing on dealing with the city's troublesome finances. Although the population was decreasing, city services remained at an all-time

This picture was taken looking south on Jos. Campau and Caniff in 1957. Note the Cunningham's drug store at left. Another Cunningham's anchored the other end of Jos. Campau at Holbrook. In the far distance, straight down Jos. Campau can be seen the distinctive Dodge Main smokestack.

The consummate politician, Mayor Albert Zak posed for this picture in 1954, apparently for a veterans' Poppy Day sale.

high. In addition to police and fire protection and trash pickup, the city provided such amenities as sweeping the sidewalks of snow and continuous street sweeping. In addition, the city employees had a pension system that had become perhaps the most generous in the nation and would have a major impact on the city's finances in years to come. Adopted in 1940, the pension system affected a mere 141 retirees and their spouses. While it cost the city $56,000 to fund it that year, by 1956 the cost was well over $300,000 and rising rapidly. Compounding the situation was that it became a common practice to promote employees to the highest level possible just before retiring so they could receive maximum benefits. On retiring, many of these people moved out of town, leaving the city in a position of paying pensions to people who were no longer supporting the tax base in any way.

Almost immediately after taking office, Zak collided with the city council over proposed employee pay increases. Zak included no increases in the $3.4 million budget he proposed to the council, citing a $464,000 budget deficit. Councilmen Henry Kozak and John Wojtylo agreed with the mayor, but the unions representing the employees, the Fraternal Order of Police, the Fire Fighters Association, and the city employees' union, Local 666, asked the council not to approve a budget that didn't include a pay hike. The council delayed approving the budget, and the employees went for more than three weeks without a payday. They got by through the unusual acquiring of "assignment sheets" from the city,

Two of Hamtramck's leading social and civic figures in the 1950s were Fr. Peter P. Walkowiak, pastor of St. Florian Parish (second from left) and Mayor Albert Zak (far right).

which were essentially vouchers that they presented to merchants, who would get the employees' checks once they were finally issued.

The issue was eventually resolved when Zak outmaneuvered the council. He vetoed the portion of the budget the council had finally approved at a meeting where there were not enough council members present to override the veto. The council members present, as well as the union officials, were seething. But Zak, a consummate politician, knew how to make the system work to his advantage. Still, these kinds of financial problems and animosity would become a routine, as Zak opposed further pay increases and the city faced more payless paydays. Zak adamantly opposed tax increases and rejected loans from the state that would have indebted the city. On the other hand, an increased property assessment in 1953 pumped $175,000 into the city's coffers.

Zak's policies and style won solid favor with the voters. He won re-election in 1954, defeating Joseph Wisniewski, 10,039 to 3,347; in 1956, easily defeating Councilman John Wojtylo by nearly 7,000 votes, 9,485 to 2,878; and in 1958, outdistancing Councilman Henry Kozak, 6,576 to 3,672 votes. Under Zak's administration, the city continued to prosper. The population decline had not had a major impact on the city yet, and indeed, there were some impressive signs of growth. In 1954, 506 stores were operating in Hamtramck. These included 127 restaurants and bars, 16 general merchandise shops, 72 apparel stores, 31 furniture and appliance stores, 25 gas stations, 17 hardware and building supply stores, 16 drug stores, and 58 miscellaneous stores. As a whole, Hamtramck's business generated $60.7 million in sales and had a payroll of $6.3 million in 1952 alone.

Some of the more favored businesses included Campau Drugs at Jos. Campau and Evaline; Modern Seat Covers at Gallagher and Holbrook; and Mazur's, Hamtramck's first and only drive-in restaurant at Comstock and Conant, which opened in 1952. Others included Barna Bee and Helen's Toyland, which was a child's vision of heaven on Jos. Campau. Off the main shopping strip were numerous corner stores, like Kucway's market and Jean's, both of which share the same side of Faber at Lumpkin. And Tony's candy store was strategically placed a block away from St. Florian School. Equally memorable, but less worth remembering, was the market that neighborhood kids unflatteringly referred to as "Moldy Joe's" on Lumpkin, where you could buy three pieces of candy for a penny. But that was about the only product the store carried since it generated most of its income from the blind pig that operated blatantly in the basement. Bars abounded. It was said that Hamtramck had more bars per capita than any city in the United States. Most were shot-and-a-beer places, like Norwalk Bar, which has remained in continuous family ownership for nearly 70 years. Some of the places had no more than a dozen seats crowded along the length of the bar. These were places for the serious drinker, who would drain a shot of Kessler's with a bottle of Goebel's, and they were places where people socialized for endless hours, arguing over politics and reliving the war.

A Christmas glow decorates Jos. Campau during an evening in the 1950s. The Ace Furniture sign at left was a familiar site on Jos. Campau for many years. Later, the building facade was covered with a gaudy gold covering. It was stripped away by the tornado of 1997, once again revealing the fine brickwork underneath.

103

The 1950s were also a time of industrial growth. Dodge Main had been expanding nearly since the day it opened, and underwent some major expansions in the 1950s. A large addition was made to the Pressed Steel Building in 1952, and at the east dock in 1956. In 1954, the city gave Chrysler land to build a pedestrian overpass over Jos. Campau. This alleviated the dangerous conditions as thousands of workers poured out of and came into the factory at the end of shift changes to get to and from the parking lots on the west side of Jos. Campau.

For decades, Dodge Main was the largest taxpayer in Hamtramck. The plant accounted for as much as one-fourth of the city's tax revenue. It provided jobs to thousands of Hamtramckans, and Chrysler made a special effort to maintain good relations with the city. Numerous times, Chrysler made early tax payments to Hamtramck so it could meet its payroll. The grateful city officials were willing to help the plant when they could. Chrysler paid for the Jos. Campau overpass, but the city gave the company a piece of land for it to bridge the street.

In November of 1954, the feelings of mutual admiration spilled out onto the streets during a week-long celebration called Dodge Days. Labeled still another "largest celebration in Hamtramck's history," the week of parties and parades drew hundreds of thousands of people to the city. Dodge used the event to showcase the new 1955 models under the slogan "Dodge has done it. Just wait!" The highlight of the event was a parade attended by Governor G. Mennen Williams behind parade marshal Roy Rogers. An estimated 70,000 people attended an open house at the plant that Sunday. Dodge Main staged a further series of "Dodge Days," which were open-houses and car shows to introduce new models. About 75,000 people attended Dodge Days in September of 1956.

But Dodge Main wasn't the only factory in town. In the 1920s, the Chevrolet Gear and Axle plant opened on the city's west side. Although it was a huge operation, and remains so even today as American Axle, only a small portion of the sprawling complex extended into Hamtramck. The overwhelming majority of the plant was, and is, in Detroit.

Another longtime Hamtramck-based business was Acme White Lead and Color Works on St. Aubin, not far from Paddy McGraw's, founded in Detroit in 1884 by William Davies and Thomas Neal, both age 26. They had drafted a plan to produce and market ready-mixed paints, a concept that was new at the time. Working with one employee, a paint mixer, they weathered a rough beginning when no orders were placed. But business steadily grew. They bought the plant on St. Aubin, and by 1896, began to expand it. Eventually, it would grow to be the single largest individual paint factory in the world, employing more than 1,000 workers. But consider the name: Acme White *Lead* and Color Works. It is synonymous with industrial pollution. Indeed, kids in the 1950s would often play among the pools of discarded chemicals and toxic materials abandoned on the huge complex, which they called "the Lab." Old laboratory buildings were filled with chemicals, including acids, and various equipment that were child-magnets. There are no records of a child being injured or suffering long-term harm from playing on the site, but after the plant closed in the 1980s and the property was

The Kowalski Sausage Company was founded in Detroit but moved to Hamtramck, on Holbrook Avenue, where the plant remains in operation today.

sold, it became the focus of a major environmental lawsuit dealing with the cleanup of the site.

Less hazardous, but equally important to the business scene, was Swedish Crucible Steel Company, on Conant, founded in 1910 by Nels Olson. In later years, it would become the Olsonite Corporation, headed by Oscar "Ozzy" Olson, who was also a prominent figure in Indy 500 racing. Olsonite, however, was best known for becoming the largest maker of toilet seats in the world.

Then there was the Kowalski Sausage Company. It has been tied to Hamtramck since Zygmund and Agnes Kowalski, who had emigrated from Poland, founded it in 1920. Originally, the Kowalskis opened a grocery store with a smokehouse at the back on Chene Street in old Poletown. They produced cured hams and the traditional Polish kielbasa. Soon, the demand grew for their aromatic kielbasa, and the Kowalskis opened the Z. Kowalski Company at 8923 Jos. Campau in Hamtramck. The Kowalski Sausage Company eventually moved to Holbrook where a block-long plant was built. It still actively operates there today.

There were other businesses as well, and in the relative boom times in the 1950s, all were doing well. Swedish Crucible, in fact, expanded in 1956. The city added to the industrial scene itself in 1957 when it broke ground for a $673,000 incinerator in the Department of Public Works yards. This had been a favorite project of Mayor Zak. The mayor also had been a strong proponent of building a new library, which was finally constructed on Caniff in 1956. The library dated back to the days of Tau Beta, before Hamtramck was even a city. Over the decades,

"The latest" in Department of Public Works equipment is displayed in the 1950s.

The Hamtramck Public Library finally got its own building in 1956. By the early 1960s, it was well established as a community resource.

the library was housed in the second story of a building, at Caniff and Jos. Campau, in the old Pilsudski School. The new one-story building would eventually be named the Albert Zak Memorial Library.

As the 1950s rolled to an end, Hamtramck was in relatively good shape. Business was thriving and projects, like the library, were signs of strength. The city remained a political powerhouse, so much so that President Harry Truman came to town three times, in 1948, 1952, and 1958. On October 12, 1958, when he participated in the Pulaski Day parade, he told his aides, "Stop this car. There are too many of my friends here. I'll get out and walk," as he drove down Jos. Campau. Dressed in a charcoal gray suit, the former president addressed the crowd for 15 minutes, noting, "We turn toward the future and hope that Polish people will once again emerge from oppression."

Truman's visit was not the only source of pride for the city. In the late 1950s and early 1960s, the city boasted two world championship baseball teams. In 1959, the Hamtramck national squad won the Little League World Series by defeating Auburn, California, 12-0. Two years later, the Hamtramck team won the Pony League World Series. These were crowning achievements of an outstanding recreation program that produced a number of champions. Hamtramck teams won 71 national titles in 11 years. The recreation program was created in 1925 and was at its peak in the 1950s and 1960s, offering a wide variety of activities,

President Harry Truman visits Hamtramck on Pulaski Day—October 12, 1958. At left is Mitchell Odrobina and to Truman's right is Governor G. Mennen Williams.

including baseball, football, tennis, basketball, bowling, wrestling, track and field, boxing, hockey, and even golf.

Of particular note were the accomplishments of tennis teacher Jean Hoxie. She and her husband, Jerry, traveled the world conducting tennis clinics, and in Hamtramck, they groomed champions. A former professional player, Jean Hoxie had attracted national attention as early as 1948 when she was featured in an article in *American Lawn Tennis* magazine. That was picked up by *Reader's Digest*, which ran it under the title "Tennis Teacher Extraordinary." Two of Hoxie's students achieved major success in the world of professional tennis. Fred Kovaleski was ranked 14th in the nation in 1954, and in 1964, 15-year-old Jane "Peaches" Bartkowicz won the Junior Girls World championship. Most of Hoxie's thousands of students over the years never played professionally or won any tournaments, but they shared in the city's great sports tradition. Hamtramck also produced several professional athletes. Steve Gromek played baseball for the Cleveland Indians and Detroit Tigers. Tom Paciorek played for the Braves, Dodgers, Mariners, White Sox, Mets, and Rangers. Other baseball pros were Bill Nahorodny, Ike Blessitt, Mike Blyzka, John Paciorek, and Ted Kazanski. Basketball fans will recognize Hall of Famer Rudy Tomjanovich for playing with

Jean Hoxie was legendary in the world of tennis for her training programs that produced champions.

Basketball Hall of Famer Rudy Tomjanovich (left) barely tops Mayor Robert Kozaren. Tomjanovich starred with the Houston Rockets in a stellar career that began at Hamtramck High School.

and coaching the Houston Rockets in the National Basketball Association. Other pro stars from Hamtramck include golfer Max Evans and world lightweight wrestling champion Walter Roxey.

On a warm summer afternoon at the baseball diamonds or tennis courts at Veterans Memorial Park, or on a chilly evening at the skating rink, the problems facing Hamtramck seemed insignificant. Nevertheless, the rich tapestry of community strength and physical infrastructure was beginning to fray. The population continued its decline, and there were more financial shortages. In July of 1957, workers had to wait two extra days to be paid because of a budget shortfall, and that was after Chrysler made a $200,000 early tax payment to avoid a payless payday. In 1958, the city was facing a $462,000 budget deficit, and there were persistent rumors that the city was deteriorating. Hamtramck's city council sought to dispel that impression by releasing a report of the city engineer that $152,167 in building permits were issued between February and April of 1957. But the city was aging, and changing.

A drastic alteration of appearance started to take place in the 1950s when Dutch elm disease was detected. For years, majestic trees canopied city streets. They formed huge arches of branches over the streets, giving them a cathedral appearance. The deadly Dutch elm beetles infected and killed the trees by the hundreds. They had to be cut down, laying the streets bare and removing the

Prior to the devastation wrought by the Dutch elm beetles, most of Hamtramck's streets were lined with majestic trees. This photo was taken in 1954 on Gallagher, just north of Casmere.

country atmosphere that had characterized the city. Nothing could be done about Dutch elm disease.

Portions of the sewer lines were more than 50 years old. Water lines and connections, some made of wood, dated nearly that far back, but there had been no sustained program to replace them. Side streets had been erratically planned. Some were nearly twice as wide as others, and there was seemingly no way to unify them. Little had been done to enforce zoning ordinances, so factories were literally next door to homes. There were no green spaces and berms to separate industry from homes. Some of the houses had deteriorated badly and were in need of major repairs, or were beyond saving and needed to be demolished. City officials had not entirely ignored these problems, but long-range planning was virtually nonexistent. Such planning was crucial to an aging city that should already have been in the redevelopment stages. In defense of the city officials, not many other towns at that time were much concerned with long-range planning either. Only in recent years has that become a standard priority among cities.

However, this shouldn't imply that Hamtramckans didn't care about the future of their town. As early as February of 1952, 60 citizens and business leaders held a meeting at the Tau Beta Community House to urge for the creation of a city planning commission. Their immediate concerns were parking and the condition of houses, not such long-range issues as zoning reform and infrastructure. The planning commission was finally formed in 1957, when Hamtramck residents approved a 1 mill tax hike for slum clearance. That was a true commitment to the future.

So, by 1960, Hamtramck was striving for its own little piece of Camelot. It was an image that would be reinforced by President John F. Kennedy, who came to Hamtramck barely a week before he was elected president. Kennedy spoke to a crowd of 5,000 at Keyworth Stadium. Although Hamtramck's population had declined by nearly 9,000 people between 1950 and 1960, and stood at 34,137, it was still a Democratic powerhouse, which Kennedy acknowledged.

"I am elated to be in the strongest Democratic city in the United States," he said. "A city which in good times and bad, in fair wind, in storm, in rain or in shine, turns out and voted Democratic and supports the progressive movement in this country." Kennedy knew his audience. Later in his speech, he noted, "In the words of the Polish National Anthem, 'As long as you live, Poland lives.' " It was an allusion that rang true with the overwhelmingly Polish voting block. Hamtramck came through for Kennedy with 14,985 votes compared to 1,521 for Richard Nixon. Kennedy would express his gratitude with a quick trip back to Hamtramck when he rolled through town in his white Lincoln Continental on October 6, 1962.

Just as President Kennedy seemed to bring a fresh breeze to the nation, Hamtramck was seeking to redevelop itself for the future. The city had already begun its urban renewal program in October of 1959 with the identification of the R-29 area, which involved removing houses on Smith and Clay Streets across

Just prior to being elected president in 1960, John F. Kennedy visited Hamtramck. (Courtesy of The Citizen.*)*

from Jos. Campau. These were the homes of some 600 African-American families. The R-30 project, also begun in the early 1960s, involved clearing houses for the I-75 expressway, which was being extended through the metro Detroit area. The route cut through the northwest section of the city, splitting off a portion, including the Colonel Hamtramck Homes, away from the main body of the city. About 220 buildings, including three churches and a business, were demolished. Also removed were about 1,200 families, nearly three-quarters of whom were African American. The last major urban renewal project was the R-31 Wyandotte Project. This program centered on the area bounded by Holbrook, Jos. Campau, Hewitt, and Lumpkin, spanning 197 parcels of property, including some city owned land.

The plan called for building a new civic center, including city hall, police station, fire station, a senior citizen residence, and housing. Plans were on track when the federal government approved an initial $1.2 million for the project, with Hamtramck providing 25 percent of the total cost of $3.1 million. It sounded like a great proposal: Hamtramck would at last have a real city hall and civic center, which it never really had before. For decades, city offices were scattered in as many as a dozen different sites across town, mainly on the second floors of

In the 1950s, momentum for the urban renewal program picked up. Here Mayor Albert Zak and city officials look over some dilapidated houses.

112

buildings along Jos. Campau. For years, the old police and fire station at Jos. Campau and Grayling had also served as a municipal building. But by the 1960s, the building was in near shambles. One person who spent time in jail recalls how he passed the hours by picking apart the crumbling brick walls of his cell, much to the agitation of the guards.

Not surprisingly, many residents were unhappy about the prospects of losing their homes. In 1965, a group of 100 residents appeared before the city council opposing the urban renewal program, but plans went on unabated. During the entire decade of the 1960s, urban renewal dominated the city's attention, as various proposals were made, then altered, then canceled. Exactly what went awry probably will never be known because the program was enveloped in shadowy dealings, claims, accusations, and rumors. But clearly something was wrong. People in the area saw perfectly good homes placed on the demolition lists. The story was that if you knew the right person, you could get the city to buy your house through the urban renewal program at an inflated price, then move to the suburbs.

To stem the opposition to the program, and retain the rich federal pot of money being made available, meetings were held with community members. At one of those meetings, someone—it isn't clear who—said that the urban renewal program should be supported because it could be used to demolish the homes of the black residents and move them out of town. Someone recorded the statement and took the tape to the University of Detroit Urban Law Center.

As the young lawyers mulled what they heard, in September of 1968, city officials met with representatives of the federal Department of Housing and Urban Development to discuss a possible $20 million grant for urban renewal. By this time, the Smith-Clay project had been completed and plans were well under way for demolishing buildings in the R-31 area. On the table was an $8-million redevelopment of the Denton-Miller area, as the first phase of the project.

"The purpose of the trip here by these HUD officials is to cut red tape and get the Neighborhood Development Program off the ground," said Charles Kotulski, urban renewal director for the city. "With our own master plan, we're actually two or more years ahead of cities that didn't anticipate these federal funds to be available."

A few weeks later, Congressman Lucien Nedzi announced that Hamtramck had been awarded a $3.8-million grant to redevelop the R-31 area.

The curtain dropped in November of 1969, when a group representing residents claiming they were displaced by the city's urban renewal program filed suit in federal district court, charging that not enough low-cost housing for African Americans was planned for the R-31 area. Known as the South End Improvement Association, the group was represented by the U-D Urban Law Center.

On its face, the charge seemed serious enough, but implications went far beyond what anyone was anticipating. Ultimately, the federal district judge would rule that Hamtramck was guilty of systematic "Negro removal" and placed an order on the city that no building could be demolished without court approval. The city appealed the decision and won a partial reversal, but the majority of the judgment stood. City officials stubbornly refused to concede wrongdoing and the case would drag on in court, incredibly, for more than 30 years. For much of that time, the city was denied any federal grants. This effectively killed the urban renewal program and wiped out all hopes of building a civic center. For years, the 40-acre tract that made up the R-31 area would remain vacant, a throwback to 70 years prior when the area was fallow fields. While the city remained adamant about not giving in to the charges, it did have a point, in that it repeatedly asked for a list of the plaintiffs who supposedly had lost their homes in the program, but the list wasn't produced.

The urban renewal program was a disaster of epic proportions, and remains perhaps the longest lawsuit in the history of the Department of Housing and Urban Development, or any other government agency. Due to the fact that productivity was stalled in so many areas because of it, Hamtramck may never be able to measure its full impact. Development in the city was virtually frozen for decades. Ironically, it would take one of the biggest developments in the United States to finally to loosen the grip of the courts, and then only a bit. And that was still 10 years off.

The 1960s brought change in other ways. Mayor Zak remained solidly popular with the Hamtramck voters, and he seemed thoroughly attached to the city. But in 1963, he took a position with Wayne County. He served as chairman of the Wayne County Civil Service Commission before being elected to the county board of supervisors. He resigned as mayor of Hamtramck and was succeeded by council president Joseph Grzecki Sr. The urban renewal program remained a priority throughout the Grzecki administration, although he also oversaw such subsequent projects as the building of the Department of Public Works building on Buffalo Street in 1965.

Even as that building was opening, one of Hamtramck's most venerable buildings was running out of time. St. Francis Hospital was getting ready to shut its door. Built in 1927 as Hamtramck Municipal Hospital, St. Francis was seen as a necessity to the growing immigrant community. There, the majority of the patients, who were Poles, could find comfort with a mainly Polish-speaking medical and support staff. In 1931, the city turned over operations of the hospital to the Sisters of St. Francis at a charge of $1 a year, and they named it St. Francis Hospital. The hospital expanded in 1935 and a public health clinic was built next door. Over the hospital's lifespan, more than 350,000 patients passed through the doors. The three-story Georgian revival building with its stately Doric half-pillars at the front door was one of Hamtramck's key institutions. The first operation performed there was an appendectomy done by Dr. Rudolph Tenerowicz, who was chief of staff for many years and for a time mayor of Hamtramck. Dr. Stephen Skrzycki, who also served as mayor, was on staff.

Thousands of the city's residents were born and died there. By the 1960s, the hospital was in terminal condition itself. While it was state of the art in 1927, the

For many years, the Gray Ladies assisted the staff at St. Francis Hospital.

St. Francis Hospital was opened as Hamtramck Municipal Hospital in 1927. It was leased to the sisters of St. Francis in 1931. They renamed it St. Francis. In 1969, it was converted to city hall, and remains in that use today.

One of the two isolation units in the basement of the hospital resembles a dungeon with its steel door.

hospital was bypassed by time and the advances of medicine. Even by 1940, it was becoming primitive. Some of its facilities would be considered shocking today, such as the two small cells with the barred windows on the door in the basement. That was where they put the drunks suffering DTs or the infectious patients with tuberculosis.

Mrs. Martha Violet Kowalski was a nurse's aide at St. Francis Hospital in 1940 and went on to become a nurse. She saw the progress of medicine over the decades and remembers St. Francis as "archaic," but the amenities were quaint.

"The nurses had to crush pills and use a Bunsen burner with some water to make medicine to put in a syringe," she recalled. "Everybody got on their tray a little pot and a little creamer. They were all metal, not this plastic junk you get now. It was beautiful. Even the trays were set up nice."

At the least, she said, the hospital was exceptionally clean, but it was also aging. The city had allocated money for routine upkeep, but by the 1950s, it was clear that the building was becoming outmoded. The Sisters of St. Francis had their collective eye on moving to a new site, north of Hamtramck, where they planned to build Holy Cross Hospital. Some city officials voiced concerns that the order was using money earmarked for St. Francis to help build Holy Cross. The sisters defended their move, saying that it was prompted by lack of demand. The obstetrics department had closed in 1963. Conversely, the hospital also had only 100 beds, making it much too small to be profitable. Costs of modernizing the building were too great for either the city or the sisters to bear, so at midnight on December 3, 1968, the hospital officially closed. The last of the patients had been moved to Holy Cross Hospital by National Guard ambulances. All that was left after midnight was night watchman Edward Kristofik, who told anyone who called that the hospital was closed for good.

Hamtramck officials did not know, then, what to do with the empty building. It was proposed that it be turned into a nursing home. Fr. Alphonse Madeja,

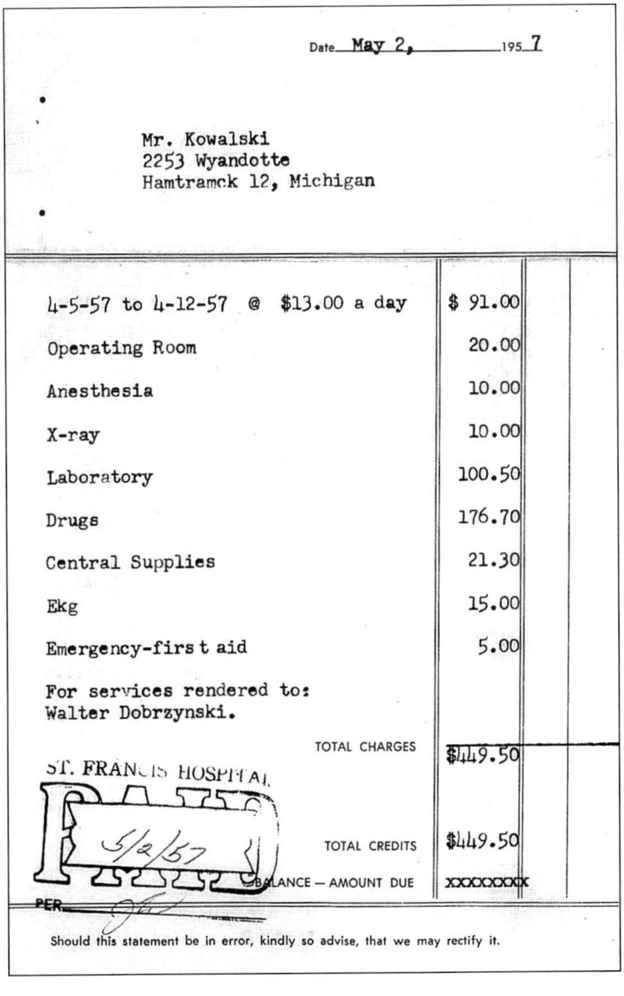

Date __May 2,_____ 195_7_

Mr. Kowalski
2253 Wyandotte
Hamtramck 12, Michigan

4-5-57 to 4-12-57 @ $13.00 a day	$ 91.00
Operating Room	20.00
Anesthesia	10.00
X-ray	10.00
Laboratory	100.50
Drugs	176.70
Central Supplies	21.30
Ekg	15.00
Emergency-first aid	5.00
For services rendered to: Walter Dobrzynski.	
TOTAL CHARGES	$449.50
TOTAL CREDITS	$449.50
BALANCE — AMOUNT DUE	XXXXXXXX

ST. FRANCIS HOSPITAL

5/2/57

PER

Should this statement be in error, kindly so advise, that we may rectify it.

It cost a whopping $13 a day to stay at St. Francis Hospital in 1957, as this patient's bill shows.

pastor of Our Lady Queen of Apostles Church, was more blunt. At a city planning commission meeting in June, he recommended that the building be razed and a new facility be erected. That became one of five proposals the planning commission ultimately settled on. Another of the options was to turn the building into a new city hall. Within a year, that proposal was realized as the majority of the city officers were gathered together in St. Francis Hospital, christened Hamtramck City Hall. It was supposed to be a temporary move until the city built a new municipal complex. More than 30 years later, St. Francis Hospital is still city hall.

Looking back on the 1960s, the view is both troubling and inspiring. Some of Hamtramck's most serious long-term problems, particularly the urban renewal lawsuit, originated in the 1960s, but it was also a time of great vitality. Hamtramckans took pride in the fact that a former Hamtramck High School star athlete had a hand in making the Apollo 11 space craft that landed on the moon in July of 1969. John Maziuk was material project coordinator for construction of the Apollo 11 command and service module for North American Rockwell Space Division. Years earlier, at Hamtramck High School, he had been a star half-mile runner.

Polish pride could not have been more evident than in September of 1969 when 49-year-old Karol Cardinal Wojtyla of Poland came to Hamtramck as part of a tour of the United States. He expressed gratitude to Poles in America for their

This picture portrays the veneration of Our Lady of Czestochowa at St. Florian Church. Such religious ceremonies have been a staple of the community since the Polish people brought their faith to the town nearly a century ago.

Students rehearse for the Hamtramck High School senior play in June 1951.

support of Poland since the end of World War II. St. Florian Church was filled to capacity as Cardinal Wojtyla said Mass after attending a banquet at the Activities Building. Cardinal Wojtyla would return to Hamtramck almost exactly 18 years later, but with a new name: Pope John Paul II.

Like the city, the public schools were undergoing change as enrollment declined. Buildings were aging and teachers were simmering about the growing disparity of their salaries compared with other districts, even with non-teachers within the district. In 1965, some Hamtramck teachers were making $1,000 less a year than the school bus drivers, who were getting $7,500. With Hamtramck's history as a solid union town, it should not have been surprising when the district's 150 teachers sought to negotiate a contract with the school board. Under the 1947 Hutchinson Act, however, the school board and administrators weren't obligated to negotiate with the teachers. So, the Hamtramck teachers took a cue from the past, and in April of 1965, they "occupied" Copernicus Junior High School, staging a sit-down strike. It was an incongruous sight as the teachers spread their blankets on the floors of the building, but it worked. Within four days, state superintendent Lyn Bartlett helped negotiate an end to the strike. The teachers union and the administrators sat down and negotiated a contract—in fact, they produced the first teachers' union contract in Michigan.

There would be further teacher labor unrest in the late 1960s, including a strike in 1969, but those were tumultuous times all over the United States. Hamtramck was sending young men to fight in Vietnam, the Civil Rights Movement was in full force, and the Dodge Main Revolutionary Movement (DRUM) was formed by militant African Americans at Dodge Main. These workers bitterly opposed Chrysler management, as well as the United Auto Workers, whom they claimed were not supporting them.

How deeply the sentiments ran is shown in this poem, written in 1969 by an anonymous Dodge Main worker:

Deep in the gloom
of the oil-filled pit
where the engine rolls down the line,
we challenge the doom
of dying in shit
while strangled by the swine . . .
. . . For hours and years
we've sweated tears
trying to break our chain . . .
But we broke our backs
and died in packs
to find our manhood slain . . .
But now we stand
for DRUM's at hand
to lead our Freedom fight,
and now 'til then
we'll unite like men . . .
For now we know our might,
and damn the plantation
and the whole Chrysler nation
for DRUM has dried our tears,
and now as we die
we've a different cry
for now we hold our spears!
U.A.W. is scum
OUR THING IS DRUM!!!!

This attitude did not spark the flames of the riot that seared Detroit in July of 1967, but it reflected the anger of the times. Hamtramck remained calm throughout the week of the riot, as city trucks were parked across the streets that crossed the border into Detroit. Nevertheless, the clouds of gray smoke from the flames that erupted in Detroit spread across Hamtramck as well.

The clouds were merely an omen of stormy days ahead.

6. SHIFTING GEARS

Hamtramck's population stood at 34,137 in 1960. Ten years later, it was down to 27,245. The decline was still not alarming, but it was telling. In 40 years, Hamtramck had lost more than half of its population, but those who remained were committed to their town. In July of 1963, Hamtramck became the fist city in the state in which the residents voted for a 1 percent income tax. The people were committed to preserve their quality of life, but the challenge was great.

No amount of money could change the fact that Hamtramck was an inner city town, completely surrounded by Detroit and subjected to the crime that spilled over its borders. Relatively, the level of crime in Hamtramck has remained low, but while some suburban communities might not record a single homicide in 20 years, evidence supports that there were most likely several happening annually. Ask Hamtramckans even today what their biggest concerns about the community are, and chances are they will say the appearance of the town—that it be maintained and kept clean. Fear of crime is not an overwhelming issue.

As the 1970s arrived, the biggest concern was money. With the declining population and reduced tax base, the city still had not come to terms with the need to reduce operating costs. It was still spending at the pace it had been decades earlier, beyond its means. The city occasionally had faced payless paydays and relied on advance tax payments from Dodge Main over the years, but in 1969, signs of serious trouble were more frequent. In April, the city had to borrow $75,000 to meet its payroll. It was only a 30-day loan at 5.5 percent, but that should not have happened with the revenue of the income tax.

"We are not broke, but we are overextended on our budget," said city comptroller Roy Kmiecik. "We started this fiscal year in balance, but the raises to the fire and the police and the raises to the city workers' union will leave us about $300,000 in deficit at the end of the fiscal year on June 30."

By June, just a few weeks before the end of the fiscal year, the projected deficit was $976,864 in the $4.2 million budget. In December, city officials called on the Chrysler Corporation for help once again in the form of an advance tax payment of $24,000 to avoid payless paydays for the holidays. By now, the state was taking notice of the city's financial problems. Even Chrysler was showing signs that its generosity was being strained. Chrysler urged the city to take advantage of advice offered by the Research Council of Michigan on how to make government operations, particularly budgets, more efficient, but little happened. And the residents took note. In the city primary election in February of 1970, incumbent Mayor Joseph Grzecki was knocked out of the running by city treasurer William Kozerski and Raymond Wojtowicz, a member of the Wayne County Community College Board of Trustees. Kozerski focused his campaign on building for the future. Wojtowicz was more direct. His campaign slogan became a mantra: "Where did the money go?"

Wojtowicz's question resonated with the Hamtramck voters and in the general election in April, he defeated Kozerski, 5,848 votes to 4,103 votes. Problems were waiting for Wojtowicz as soon as he entered his office. The Michigan Municipal Finance Commission had ordered the city to produce a balanced budget, and while it approved the city's request for a $400,000 tax anticipation loan, it also put the city on notice that costs had to be controlled—even if that meant steep cuts of staff and service. Wojtowicz began a campaign to clean up the city's finances. Within days of taking office, he asked the state attorney general to conduct an audit of the city's finances.

A few weeks later, Michigan deputy treasurer James Marling summed up the city's finances as being "a mess." In response, Wojtowicz called for the laying off of 125 city employees, as there was no money to meet the payrolls. Part of the blame for the financial shortfall was attributed to the city's extremely generous pension system. "Your pension eligibility must be altered as soon as possible," Marling said. To reinforce the seriousness of the situation, the state took over control of the city's finances. In the same address to the council on Tuesday, May 19, 1971, in which Marling said the city was in deep financial trouble, he would utter the words that would become locally legendary: "You can't even buy a pencil without state approval."

The council wrestled with a budget that ultimately included the layoff of 69 employees. Almost immediately, the Hamtramck Homeowners Association began a campaign to recall four city council members blamed for delaying the adoption of the budget and mishandling the city's finances.

Association president Ted Marecki charged the council members with "blundering and non-feasance." In short, the people of Hamtramck were furious with the council's continued ineptitude and discernible inability to recognize and deal with its own problems. Due to legal maneuvering by the targeted council members, the recall election did not take place until January of 1972, but when it did finally occur, the four council members were easily turned out of office.

"Congratulations, Hamtramck!" screamed the headline on *The Citizen* newspaper on January 27, 1972. It may not have been an example of impartial journalism, but it did reflect the overall mood of the people. Technically, the recall was based on the charges that the four councilpersons had mismanaged money, including paying a $300,000 bill for the festering urban renewal project against the advice of city attorney Edmund Torcellini. They were also charged with refusing to accept free labor to help the poor through a work program offered by Wayne

Mayor Raymond Wojtowicz was up to his elbows in work, trying to straighten out Hamtramck's troubled finances that reached the breaking point in the early 1970s. (Courtesy of The Citizen.)

County. Governor William Milliken immediately appointed Robert Zwolak, Michael Mozola, David Zukowski, and Mitchell Lewandowski to fill the vacancies created by the recall. All had been involved in some way in the city activities and organizations over the preceding years, but the voters viewed them as a collective stopgap, and a brief one at that. In elections held the following May, three of the council appointees were replaced by newcomers. Only Michael Mozola would retain his seat.

While the city government appeared to be in shambles as the recall played out, the city life itself continued on as always, seemingly insulated from the manic machinations in city hall. Most significantly, in April of 1972, all of Hamtramck joined together in a huge celebration to mark the 50th anniversary of incorporation as a city. Nearly 600 persons attended a banquet at the Knights of Columbus Hall on Conant. Among those attending were Congressman Lucien Nedzi; John Riccardo, president of Chrysler Corporation; Congressman Stanley Rozycki; state senator Ted Mrozowski; Detroit assessor Stanley Gruszkowski; and George Chick, representing Highland Park. As part of the program, Mayor Wojtowicz unveiled Hamtramck's first official flag. Designed by St. Ladislaus student Michael Balabuch, the flag features the city seal on a silver and white background. The silver was especially significant because it implied steel, the stuff of the auto industry, which made modern Hamtramck.

Revelers partied in the street below the impressive spire of St. Florian Church in the distance during the city's 50th anniversary celebration.

Thousands of people poured onto the streets to mark Hamtramck's 50th anniversary as a city in June 1972. Since then, many of the stores pictured here have gone, replaced by others in the constantly changing cityscape.

As part of the celebration, a special Mass attended by 500 people was held at St. Florian, but the real fun was yet to come. In June, the city staged a gigantic weekend birthday celebration, attended by a staggering 250,000 people or so. Former residents came back home as people literally danced in the streets. It was as if all the city's problems had vanished. People wanted to have fun, and they wanted to remember that, despite its fiscal woes, Hamtramck was still a city they could be proud of. Even those who had long since moved away viewed Hamtramck as the old hometown. It generated countless memories. Besides, Hamtramckans always knew how to have a good time, even under the worst conditions. And to a degree, the worst was over. The city would still wrangle with the state over the budget, and the teachers went on strike again the following September, but by the 50th anniversary celebration, it appeared that Hamtramck would weather the storm.

The city got another morale boost that October when Hollywood came to Hamtramck. Gene Hackman and Al Pacino, and a production crew of 40, came to town to film scenes for their movie *Scarecrow*. Hamtramck was chosen because some of the characters in the film have Polish family connections and the producers wanted an authentic Polish-American city as a backdrop. The climax scene of the film was shot at a telephone booth at Lumpkin and Caniff. Years later, Hackman would recall his experience filming in Hamtramck as one of the favorite moments in his distinguished career.

That wasn't the only film shot in Hamtramck either. In 1977, Richard Pryor and Harvey Keitel came to a house on Lehman Street to film scenes for the movie *Blue Collar*. And the 1998 production of *Polish Wedding*, starring Claire Daines and Lena Olin, was filmed almost entirely in Hamtramck, especially using Wyandotte Street as a backdrop.

Back in the real world, Wojtowicz wrestled with bringing the city back on an even financial keel with the help of city advisers. The layoffs did not sit well with city employees and a powerful contingent built up against Wojtowicz. Plus, Al Zak had re-entered the political stage after 10 years out of office while he served with the county. Zak, who lived his whole life in the same house in Hamtramck, said he had been urged by residents to run again and bring stability to the city. "Bring Zak Back" was the campaign cry. He railed against the mismanagement of the urban renewal program and the general state of affairs. Zak said the people were disgusted and did not know who to blame for the situation. Zak was banking on the fact that the citizens would blame Wojtowicz, and he was right to an extent. Zak outpolled Wojtowicz 3,637 to 2,645 in the primary election and 4,409 to 4,239 in the general election. In reality, Wojtowicz was in a no-win situation. He had to cut jobs and trim services to save money, but that raised the ire of the city workers' union, which was still a powerful voting block. He also had to deal with a hostile city council until the four members were recalled.

Many voters saw in Zak a return to the old days of Hamtramck. Under Zak's earlier tenure, Hamtramck boasted clean streets and paved alleys. Life in Hamtramck was good. What the people did not notice in the 1950s was that little

The film Battle Circus *playing at the Farnum Theater dates this photo to 1953. The theater was torn down in the late 1960s.*

was actually being done to handle the financial problems that were sure to rise in the future. It was clear even then that the city workers' pension system was bleeding the city, and there wasn't going to be enough money in the future.

Zak's sudden death the following year ended any question about what he would accomplish in office. Council president William V. Kozerski, who had been involved in politics for nearly 20 years, including serving as city treasurer and a councilman, succeeded him.

The mid- to late-1970s was a period of relative calm in Hamtramck. There were no major financial disasters and the political scene, while always boisterous, was comatose compared with the earlier years of the decade. While it was not a period of setbacks, neither was it a period of growth. Instead, the population kept shrinking and the luster of the Jos. Campau shopping district began to seriously fade. Neisner's, Grant's and Kresge's all closed, as did Max's Jewelry, along with many of the fine clothing stores. Farnum Theater had been demolished in 1969 and Martha Washington, the last of the city's movie houses, was in financial trouble. In 1979, the city's shopping district suffered a major blow with the closing of Federal's department store, although that was due to the collapse of the Federal's company and had nothing directly to do with any changes in Hamtramck. Still, there were a few bright spots. The school district built a new community center in 1979 and developer Henry Velleman realized that Jos. Campau still had a lot of a lot of potential. He began buying buildings around the city and renovated them.

And then the bomb dropped.

In June of 1979, Chrysler squelched rumors that it was planning to close the Dodge Main plant by announcing that it was going to do just that. Chrysler was in desperate financial shape at the time and was appealing to the federal government for a bailout loan. The company knew that if it was to be transformed into a successful company, it would have to cut costs and modernize.

Dodge Main was old and cost too much to operate, $14 million a year. The gigantic plant had been constructed in pieces, with buildings being added to and on top of other buildings over its entire lifetime. It had grown into a multi-story complex made up of nearly three dozen buildings covering 100 acres. Modern car making called for assembly to be streamlined on one floor. Much of Dodge Main still had wooden block floors that had been obsolete for decades.

To Hamtramck, the closing of Dodge Main was devastating. The city stood to lose about $1.4 million in tax revenue with the closing of the plant. With a budget of $8.8 million, the loss was crippling. And then there was the question of what to do with the mammoth plant. Built of concrete and steel, it was expected to last a millennium. Detroit was already littered with the carcasses of dead factories and it looked like Hamtramck was going to add to their shadows. Mayor Kozerski tried to hush the alarm with words of encouragement that Hamtramck had suffered through worse, although it would be hard to identify when. City officials

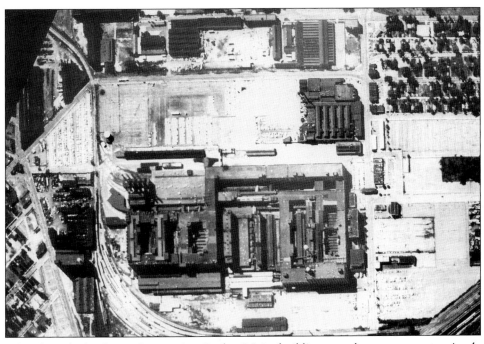

Seen from high above, the massive Dodge Main building complex appears as a simple rectangle. In reality, it covered 5 million square feet of floor space spread out in more than 30 buildings rising up to eight stories high. North is at bottom. Jos. Campau is at right.

During the turbulent 1960s, civil rights consciousness began to rise. The Hamtramck NAACP staged this parade on Jos. Campau.

were angry that they had not been informed of the closing until just before the official announcement was made. The UAW chimed in with the following:

> Chrysler's plan to close this plant and throw thousands of Chrysler workers out on the street permanently is short-sighted and unnecessary. Even if economic circumstances require the corporation to reduce production for the time being, the problem could be handled in a manner which would not require all of the burden to be borne by the workers in this one plant.

Further rallies were held, including an NAACP parade down Jos. Campau, but Chrysler was unmoved, or perhaps it would be more fair to say, it couldn't afford to be moved. With Chrysler teetering on the verge of bankruptcy, it had to take drastic action to save itself. The plant was to close by the following January. Shutting down Dodge Main wasn't just Hamtramck's problem. Thousands of people were going to lose their jobs, and that would affect the regional economy as a whole.

Soon, ripples of the plant's closing began to spread nationally, and even internationally. The plight of Hamtramck was being cast as the epitome of what was wrong with American industry and symbolized the spreading rust belt. The *Washington Post* and *New York Times* sent reporters to Hamtramck to do stories, which seemed more like obituaries. Documentary film crews from Great Britain and Germany came to film Hamtramck's situation.

By August, the state, county, and local officials proposed a $1-million grant for the city. Chrysler contributed to the fund with $50,000, along with Ford, which put in $75,000, and General Motors, which added $90,000. The money was to be used to find ways to reuse portions of Dodge Main and explore other opportunities. However, that could not stem the continuing problems with Hamtramck's fragile budget, and in September, 83 city employees were laid off.

It was not a good situation for Mayor Kozerski. While he had won election after completing Zak's term in 1975, and re-election in 1977, the situation in the city had changed drastically. City council president and former deputy city clerk Robert Kozaren capitalized on the changing conditions and pulled an upset by beating Kozerski by a nearly two-to-one margin in the August 1979 primary. Kozaren skillfully promoted a message of hope and renewal. He insisted that Hamtramck had resources in its people that had not been tapped and that the city was far from facing ruin. It was just the message that Hamtramckans wanted to hear. Kozaren carried his winning momentum to the general election in November and won by another decisive margin, 3,935 votes to Kozerski's 2,415 votes. An even more stunning upset was the defeat of city clerk Walter Gajewski, who had held the office for 29 years, by Robert Zwolak, who had been one of the appointed interim councilmen following the 1970 recall.

Standing nearly 6 foot, 6 inches, Kozaren was easy to spot as he walked down Jos. Campau, which he often did. In fact, he made a point of being easily accessible and would listen to the people who stopped him on the streets. Kozaren used his outgoing personality and his seemingly unending enthusiasm for Hamtramck to build a wide base of support. He made Hamtramckans feel proud and confident again, and refused to accept the reports of the city's supposedly approaching death.

The reality of his challenge was made physical on January 4, 1980, at about 3 p.m., when the last workers straggled out of Dodge Main. "It's a sad day," was a repeated comment. Some former employees came to the gates of the plant on Jos. Campau to pay their last respects.

When Kozaren took office in January of 1980, the city was in a desperate financial state. A $350,000 budget deficit was looming. That wasn't a new scenario, but this time there would be no Dodge Main to come through with tax advances to avoid payless paydays, and there was every indication that such days were coming. But action was being taken. In February, Kozaren led a group of city officials into the Oval Office in the White House to meet with President Jimmy Carter. The meeting had been arranged by state Senator John Hertel to emphasize the plight of Hamtramck. The federal government was already aware of the situation and President Carter dispatched an emergency task force to the city to help with revitalization.

The Department of Housing and Urban Development approved a $200,000 grant to refurbish Jos. Campau. Decorative sidewalks and new street lights would be installed along the roadway. Awnings and façade improvements were also proposed. All of this was laid out to a crowd of about 180 merchants at a special meeting called by Kozaren and the Wilkins and Wheaton engineering firm hired to do the work. Even as the program began, Governor Milliken and Senator Hertel made a tour of the city in a show of support. On the heels of that, the Department of Housing and Urban Development approved a $525,000 grant for the city. Not long afterwards, the federal Economic Development Administration gave the city a $608,000 grant. The city had lost out on a lot of grant money over the years because of the restrictions of the long-standing urban renewal lawsuit, but in the face of the Dodge Main disaster, the money freeze was beginning to thaw.

At last there was a sense of hope spreading around town that somehow Hamtramck would survive the loss of Dodge Main. With state and federal officials operating out of city hall, much-needed professional help was engineering some semblance of a recovery plan. Kozaren built on this optimism by announcing plans in April for a city festival to be held in fall. Over the years, the festival would grow to huge proportions, drawing hundreds of thousands of people to Hamtramck. This added to the already popular Strawberry Festival held each May at St. Florian parish. The Strawberry Festival itself was so popular that soon parishes around the metro area were promoting all manner of fruit for their festivals.

Also bolstering the feel-good spirit of the city, Hamtramck began to polish its image through a public relations campaign funded by a portion of the grant money. A public relations consultant was hired and decorative signs were placed around town with the word "Welcome" in several languages represented in the city. Bumper stickers were printed with the slogan "A Touch of Europe in America." While the slogan reflected the predominantly Polish and Ukrainian community, it was only a partially accurate statement, as was pointed out by some non-European residents. Along with the long-present African-American population, Hamtramck, and especially the surrounding Detroit area, was increasingly becoming the home for different ethnic groups such as Arabs and Bangladeshis.

No one wanted to raise much of an issue over not being mentioned. The most important element to Hamtramck's survival would be that it move forward, building on whatever strengths it had. Even Ronald Reagan added to the excitement by paying a campaign visit to the city in May of 1980.

Still, a year after Chrysler announced that Dodge Main was closing, and six months after that had happened, the factory loomed over the South End of town like a gigantic tombstone. Weeds forced their way up through cracks in the vast empty parking lots. Broken windows gaped along the façade. And perhaps above all, it was quiet. The sounds of heavy machinery were gone. Where thousands of workers once walked, talked, and toiled, there was only the breeze. An eerie stillness settled over the massive complex, and there was an overbearing sense of decay. Demolition was out of the question. Estimates to tear down the building ranged from $18 million to $30 million, and not even the federal government seemed inclined to commit that amount of money. Even if the building was demolished, what then? The city would be left with a 100-plus acre empty lot with no one interested in redeveloping it. So while there had been signs of improvement, the patient was still seriously, perhaps terminally, ill.

And then General Motors prescribed a cure. In June of 1980, GM announced plans to build a massive, 3 million-square-foot Cadillac assembly plant on a 500-acre parcel straddling the Detroit-Hamtramck border, including the land occupied by Dodge Main. GM had considered a variety of sites around the metro area, but none met its needs except the Detroit-Hamtramck site. Dodge Main was centrally located near the intersection of two major freeways and was already fed by a complex of rail lines. On the Detroit side of the site, the neighborhood was particularly old and run down. Many of the residents were renters, not property owners, so acquiring the huge amount of property that would be needed was more feasible. Detroit promoted the plant as a way to provide new jobs while clearing out a troubled neighborhood that no longer was viable.

Hamtramck officials were elated at the news of the new plant. Mayor Kozaren called it "a miracle." The project promised to at once solve the two most serious problems facing the city—what to do with Dodge Main and how to replace the revenue it lost when the plant closed.

Nonetheless, there were still enormous problems to overcome even before the GM plant could be built. An estimated 1,500 homes, shops, a hospital, two churches, a cemetery, 17 factories, and miscellaneous other buildings would have to be acquired and demolished. And not just torn down. The land would have to be taken back to a pristine state, which meant removing sewers and water lines, and ripping up streets, not to mention that the behemoth that was Dodge Main would have to be virtually erased without a trace left. It was a project of staggering

Mayor Robert Kozaren brought a new enthusiasm to the city after the closing of Dodge Main.

proportions and seemingly overwhelming obstacles. On top of that, GM set a deadline of one year to acquire and clear the land in preparation for construction.

Other than Dodge Main, few buildings in Hamtramck would be demolished. Most of the city's portion of the site was occupied by Dodge Main, along with some miscellaneous businesses. However, all of those buildings were critical, since Hamtramck was still under a court order stemming from the urban renewal lawsuit forbidding the city from demolishing most buildings without court approval.

Thankfully, Kozaren had worked hard to establish working relations with Detroit and was on good terms with Detroit mayor Coleman Young, and Young very much wanted the GM plant, as did Governor Milliken. Kozaren likened Young, Milliken, and GM to three knights who came to Hamtramck's rescue as intense negotiations began with federal district court judge Damon Keith. Keith had handed down the original "Negro removal" ruling.

Ultimately, the way was cleared to demolish Dodge Main. Not surprisingly, few people opposed the project in Hamtramck, but it was a different story on Detroit's side of the border. Much of the site covered the old Poletown area of Detroit, which was still dear to many residents with strong and long family ties. These residents bitterly protested plans to destroy their neighborhood. Soon, GM's then-familiar slogan of "GM—Mark of Distinction" was distorted into "GM—Mark of Destruction." It was a public relations nightmare for the world's largest auto maker, especially when demolitions actually began, but GM had the solid support of Mayor Young and Mayor Kozaren, as well as Governor Milliken.

Past and present coexist quietly in Beth-olem Cemetery. Created in 1871, the tiny cemetery was incorporated into the grounds of the GM Cadillac assembly plant, which looms over the tombstones.

Hamtramck City Council members Frank Rembisz, Eugene Pluto, Paul Ordrobina, Helen Justewicz, and Jerry Wandolowski also threw their unanimous support behind the plan. Throughout the project, they would demonstrate a unity that was seldom seen in the council chambers, and it was loudly noted that the new plant would create 6,000 new jobs. GM board chairman Thomas Murphy addressed the Hamtramck Rotary Club in November of 1981, promoting the project as a "significant asset" to Hamtramck and Detroit. He was singing to the choir. But at another church, Immaculate Conception, just off of East Grand Boulevard, opposition to the plant was mounting.

GM was being portrayed as a neighborhood destroyer, a corporation that would tear down a community church for the sake of profits. In fact, the neighborhood had been economically depressed for years and had long since lost any meaningful connection to the Poletown label. Nevertheless, protesters would later gather at the church as demolition took place in the span of one carefully planned and executed night. The nighttime destruction raised a fierce protest, including some emotional demonstrations by persons who had never even seen the church before. Also, two attorneys vowed to declare "World War III" against Detroit over the way it was acquiring the businesses to be removed. Yet, many business owners were happy to take the money and get out of town.

The most serious challenge was leveled by the Poletown Neighborhood Council, which was made up of residents in the affected area. They sought to have Hamtramck cut off from federal grants needed for the project. Before the plant could be built, it was necessary for an Environmental Impact Statement to be prepared, gauging what effect the project would have. The Neighborhood Council contended that the EIS didn't properly consider the other sites that had been proposed for the factory. The complaint contended:

> The EIS totally ignores other reasonable alternatives for reducing the size of the site. A substantial portion of the site is devoted to such auxiliary facilities as a power plant and a storm water retention pond. The EIS should have considered the possibility of moving one or both of these facilities off of the proposed site, particularly since there is contiguous and minimally utilized land available at the periphery of the proposed site.

Within days, however, the Neighborhood Council backtracked, withdrawing its objections, saying Hamtramck was targeted in error. It really didn't matter. The state Supreme Court had already ruled that the project was legal. It was going forward with the steady pace of an assembly line.

The Chrysler Corporation was among the businesses leaving town as the project progressed, although it pocketed only $1 in the deal for its sale of Dodge Main. Even so, it was a bargain. Chrysler was freed of the property taxes it still would have had to pay while the plant was standing. By November, Chrysler had stripped the plant of all valuable machinery and such amenities as the fine wood

Shortly before demolition began, Mayor Robert Kozaren led a group of city, state and Chrysler officials through Dodge Main.

paneling that the Dodge brothers had installed in an office. The historical "DB" initials on the wrought iron gates were also removed. But vast amounts of material were left behind. These ranged from car dashboards, to slide projectors, to laboratory equipment, to empty liquor bottles left on the roof, and thousands, perhaps millions, of documents. Kozaren, who always had a sense of the city's history, had a portion of the old plant's fence removed for later use to enclose a park on Jos. Campau honoring Pope John Paul II.

Shortly before the plant was abandoned, Mayor Kozaren led a small group of city officials and a few guests on a tour of it. It was both awesome and overwhelming. The vastness of the factory complex couldn't be realized from outside its walls. Only inside, overshadowed by the cavernous hallways and among the towering machinery could one get a sense of the power that once was present. A wall was studded with huge circuit breakers. The boilers looked large enough to power a battleship. And the vacant assembly buildings stretched far into the distance, with the far walls the length of three football fields. There were incongruities. Someone had spray painted the word "help" on an office window. A small building on the roof was draped with steel cables. A Chrysler official said it was "the tornado" shack that was manned during severe storms to watch for tornadoes. None were ever spotted from it, which is just as well, for when a tornado finally did strike, it surely would have sent the shack flying, along with anyone in it, had the shack still been there. On this cold December morning, the sky was bright and clear. The sunlight created a patchwork of glowing squares along the floors of the buildings. Farther inside, however, darkness ruled. The lights deep within the plant were gone, so huge pools of darkness covered floors and obliterated the entire interiors of huge buildings. The paint shop, and a host of other buildings deep within the complex, stood in silence like a tomb.

Indeed, it was the silence that was the most powerful feature of the factory. This place had been imbued with decades of the sounds of crashing machinery, creaking assembly lines and conveyors, and the voices of multitudes of workers. Even in the silence, the presence of all those who had worked there could be felt. The gigantic complex had acquired a presence all its own.

It began to disappear almost without notice as Chrylser officials walked out the doors and never returned. For 70 years, Dodge Main had been synonymous with Hamtramck. Its thudding machinery was the heart of the city. The revenue generated was its blood, and the way it touched so many thousands of lives, for better and for worse, was its soul. It is perhaps the greatest irony that the death of Dodge Main would fuel the rebirth of Hamtramck. It's almost as if the old plant gave its last gasp to save the city it grew up with. It even got the seemingly perpetual urban renewal case moving.

As plans for the GM plant were materializing, timing became even more critical. A key element of the plan was the use of a $35-million Urban Development Action Grant the city needed to demolish Dodge Main and the surrounding buildings. Without that, the project was frozen. Detroit, Hamtramck, and GM desperately needed to loosen the logjam that had stopped the urban renewal case cold for years. A special meeting was called with representatives of the plaintiffs in the case, but when that reached an impasse, federal judge Damon Keith stepped in. He called all parties to his office for a marathon negotiation session in December of 1981, and when it was over, a settlement had been reached. It included a plan to build 350 housing units in the city, 200 designated for senior citizens, and 150 for low-income persons. To oversee the development, two "corporations" of representatives of the city and the plaintiffs were formed. One corporation had jurisdiction over the R-31 (Wyandotte-Geimer-Hewitt Streets) area while the other was in charge of the Dyar-Grand Haven area, near the Colonel Hamtramck Homes, which had been seen as the site to build new homes.

"This paves the way and opens new avenues that we've been barred from," said Mayor Kozaren. In reality, the settlement actually resolved little. No houses were built, although a senior citizen complex would go up on Holbrook at the far northeast end of the R-31 area. It would still be another 20 years before any more significant progress would be made toward settling the case once and for all, but that agreement was enough to ensure that the GM plant would go up on the space occupied by Dodge Main.

Just weeks later, on a cold morning in January of 1982, cranes from the Adamo wrecking company quietly slipped into Hamtramck and took their place at the south end of one of the assembly buildings. Hoisting steel balls weighing 10,000

135

pounds and 5,000 pounds, they began chipping away at the massive plant. And so began one of the biggest demolition projects in the world. It would take about a year to tear down the factory. The scale of the project was incredible. Dodge Main covered 5 million square feet and was mainly constructed of concrete reinforced by steel rods. It would take two or three hits by a 10,000 pound wrecking ball to topple each of the hundreds of columns that supported the main floors, but the work went on relentlessly, and gradually the complex began to crumble. More equipment was moved in over the months, and the site began to resemble a war zone. Indeed, as the area was cleared of residents and sealed off, the vast stretch began to take on a surreal atmosphere. Houses were crushed literally in a matter of minutes as bulldozers rolled through them. Slowly, the horizon began to lower as whole blocks were reduced to empty fields of dirt. On Jos. Campau, across from Dodge Main, stood a block of buildings including the infamous Berkshire Motel, which was somewhat like the modern successor of Paddy McGraw's. The buildings were still occupied as demolition of Dodge Main picked up momentum. Seated in one of the bars across from the factory, one could feel the ground shake each time a wrecking ball made contact with a column several hundred feet away. But soon, those buildings were vacated and Jos. Campau was sealed. The pedestrian overpass was brought down and straddled the street until it was broken apart and hauled away. Massive cranes were brought in to pull the giant boilers from the powerhouse. And early on a Sunday morning, the four gigantic towering smokestacks were brought down.

Demolition of Dodge Main began at the far south assembly line building in 1981. Gradually more wrecking equipment would be brought in as the demolition pushed north through the massive complex.

Early one day, wreckers toppled the gigantic smokestacks that stood above the powerhouse.

As the wreckers progressed through the site, the extent of the demolition took on awesome proportions. The landscape turned into a vast distance of debris.

Who was Johann George? We likely will never know. His tombstone was unearthed by demolition crews clearing away the northeast end of the Dodge Main site.

Day by day, the workers pushed northward across the Dodge Main site and the plant got smaller. By August, all that was left was a crisscross maze of concrete foundation walls. Soon, even these would be gone, leaving a gigantic open plain. As part of the project, Paddy McGraw's long-abandoned building alongside the railroad tracks was demolished. With the roads removed and tracks realigned for the new plant, it became difficult to even remember where buildings used to be. The only mark of the past was the old Beth-olem Cemetery, located across from Dodge Main. GM officials concluded that trying to move the cemetery would be too expensive and might generate objections from the Jewish community. It's one thing to displace the living; it's quite another to disturb the dead. The cemetery would be incorporated into the new GM plant, where it still rests, at the remote northwest section of the plant grounds. Not quite visible from the surrounding road, it can be placed by the tight clump of trees that stands apart from all the rest.

Concerns of the dead also came to light in an unusual way in August when work crews unearthed the tombstone near Conant and Denton of a Johann George, dated 1886, and with an inscription in German. It was a reminder of Hamtramck's early German population and may have been found on the site of an old cemetery, but no other tombstones were found, and no records indicate a cemetery there. Johann George was destined to remain an enigma.

As demolition of the area was nearing an end, construction crews began building the Cadillac assembly plant. Much to the chagrin of GM, the plant was immediately and unofficially christened the Poletown plant, a name that has stuck. On the other hand, a name sent to oblivion was Dodge Local 3, the landmark union local that dated to the 1930s and the sit-down strike. With no more Dodge Main, there would be no more Local 3. Even the union hall near the viaduct on Jos. Campau, which saw so much history over the decades, was demolished. Part of Hamtramck's history was slipping away, piece by piece.

Meanwhile, Mayor Kozaren was making history. His first term was unparalleled in Hamtramck. The city had gone from the depths of depression to the heights of elation. Its fortunes turned around completely as nearly each day brought some new development, good and bad. It was mostly good, and by the time elections rolled again in summer of 1981, Kozaren became the first Hamtramck mayor to run unopposed. Who could follow that act? His name alone on the mayor's portion of the November ballot still gathered 4,848 votes. Only Joseph Grzecki Jr., son of the former mayor, came close to garnering Kozaren's numbers. Also running unopposed in the city treasurer's race, he had tallied 4,492 votes.

Much of Kozaren's success could be attributed to circumstances. The closing of Dodge Main, closely followed by the announcement of the GM plant, were issues largely beyond his control. Yet, Kozaren's policy of bridge building and establishing relationships were important factors in Hamtramck pulling in the

Fire destroyed the ornate Holbrook-Jos. Campau building in the early 1990s. Its loss was a blow to the cityscape, although the miniature Statue of Liberty that adorned the top (not visible here) was saved.

139

GM plant. Kozaren had worked with the plaintiffs in the urban renewal case to build a sense of trust even before the GM plant was proposed. That event was instrumental in getting the court to lift its demolition restrictions, which would have flatly killed the project. Kozaren stroked the local and national politicians to push the project ahead. Of course, he didn't do it alone. The city council showed unusual restraint and a refreshingly cooperative spirit in dealing with all the issues that had to be settled to facilitate the project. No one wanted to sour the best deal in Hamtramck's history. Kozaren rode the crest of success for 18 years, becoming the longest-serving mayor, by far, in the city's history.

In the wake of all that occurred in the first two years of the decade, all that followed in the remaining eight seemed anticlimactic. Progress was made in certain areas while the city suffered setbacks in others. The city was not greatly impacted by either. A plan to buy the old Tau Beta Community House fell through and the Acme White Lead Company site was sold to another company, which discovered (surprise!) that the land was contaminated. That led to more lawsuits. Also, Martha Washington Theatre flickered out of existence in the early 1980s to be replaced by a Wendy's fast food restaurant. Another victim of the changing times was the ornate Holbrook-Campau building, with its miniature Statue of Liberty adorning the façade.

But there were successes as well. The renovation of stores on Jos. Campau continued, and in 1982, the area of Hamtramck bordered by Holbrook, the Jos. Campau alley, Yemans, and Dequindre was named a National Historic District. This area, which includes St. Florian parish, typifies the "old" Hamtramck, with its tidy homes on tiny lots. Construction of the Hamtramck Town Center shopping mall began at Holbrook and Jos. Campau. While that area was still a mud-soaked lot, Hamtramck came into the national spotlight again in September of 1987, when Pope John Paul II returned for an official papal visit. An enormous stage was erected at the Town Center site in preparation for the pope's visit. Once again, thousands of persons turned out to greet him. The streets of Hamtramck were crowded all through the night of September 16 and 17 in anticipation of the pope's visit. People crowded into the mini-"Pope Park" at Jos. Campau and Belmont, where a huge statue of the pope had been erected a few years before, hoping to get a glimpse of the pope as he drove by.

Security was extremely tight as guards patrolled the streets. Plus, the dire predictions of mammoth traffic jams may have contributed to the crowds that turned out to hear the pope speak being smaller than expected. That made the viewing only better for those who huddled toward the stage for an up-close viewing of the pope—their pope, the man from Poland who spoke their language. They felt as if he were family, and to some he was. Former Hamtramck city Councilman John Wojtylo, who had been in office in the 1940s and 1950s, was a cousin of Karol Wojtyla, who became Pope John Paul II.

Despite a steady drizzle, no one was disappointed as the pope drove south on Jos. Campau in the confines of his bullet-proof "Popemobile." He was presented with the traditional Polish welcoming gift of bread and salt. Then he spoke:

In the course of my lengthy pilgrimage to the church in the United States God has led me to Detroit, the second largest community of people of Polish origin after Chicago. And here I am in Hamtramck, the city I know very well.

The words set the tone for the town. Hamtramck could once again take pride in itself and its ability to overcome all the adversities and problems that were presented to it. But in a sense, the pope's visit was heralding the end of another chapter in Hamtramck's history, for as he addressed the crowds in Polish, for the first time he was speaking to the minority of the city's population.

Pope John Paul II meets with the crowds as he visits Hamtramck in September 1987. (Courtesy of The Citizen.)

7. THE NEW MODEL

The Taj Mahal restaurant opened on Caniff Street. The Gandhi restaurant is on Conant Avenue, not far from the Rima Sari Center on Conant, which specializes in traditional Indian clothes. At the King Video store, John Travolta shares shelf space with a wide variety of Albanian, Bosnian, Indian, and Arab films. The Yemeni-American Association is on the south side of town, just blocks away from Holbrook Elementary School, where almost all the students are Muslim. But perhaps the most striking example of Hamtramck's melding cultures is shown by the "Café India and Coney Island" on Conant.

There are still many Polish people in Hamtramck, but they no longer make up the majority. Just as the Poles supplanted the Germans nearly a century ago, so are they being replaced by a new influx of immigrants, mainly Arabs, Bengalis, and Eastern Europeans, including Bosnians, Yugoslavians, and Albanians.

They were responsible for the population turnaround of the city. The 1980 census put Hamtramck's population at 21,300. By 1990, the figure was down to 18,372, and the numbers were looking grim going into the decade. The steadily declining population was a sign that Hamtramck was turning back into a minor village, overshadowed by Detroit. This was a demoralizing state, but it would also have a practical impact. State revenue sharing, which is vital to a small city like Hamtramck, is based on population. Fewer people mean less money, and for perpetually cash-strapped Hamtramck, that was a formula for disaster. As the 2000 census approached, fears were growing that Hamtramck's population would drop below 14,000, the lowest it had been since not long after Dodge Main had opened in 1910. Still, there were some indications that the numbers might be higher than anticipated. It seemed like a lot of people were moving into Hamtramck, even though most were immigrants who kept close to home. Often, neighbors not only did not know who was living next door, but could not even tell how many people were occupying a building. The new residents led a quiet existence, not interacting much with their neighbors as they adapted in varying degrees to contemporary American society.

Regardless, they were counted by the census, or at least many of them were, and when the numbers were officially tallied, it became clear that Hamtramck's population hadn't shrunk. In fact, it had grown—greatly. The official 2000 count was 22,976, an increase of nearly 25 percent. It was the greatest population growth of any community in Wayne County. Hamtramck was a city again as it reversed 70 years of decline, and the signs were that the growth would continue well into the next century.

What happened? How does an inner-city community, completely surrounded by perhaps the most troubled major city in the United States, keep defying the odds and insist on not just surviving, but thriving?

The answer is in the people. Despite the most outrageous actions of the city leaders over the years, and the intensity of the problems the city had encountered, the people have kept the community on an even keel. The city, as we've noted before, survives in spite of itself.

Ten years after the announcement was made that Dodge Main would be demolished, there was virtually nothing left of the plant. Only three battered signs on Conant stood, barely noticeable in small weed-filled parking lots. "Employee parking" they noted in white letters on blue metal. And that was it. Seventy years of Hamtramck's soul was reduced to three rusting signs. So thoroughly had Dodge Main been demolished that it was difficult to tell anymore where the plant had stood. A new road, Hamtramck Drive, was placed just south of the viaduct to carry traffic on Jos. Campau either east or west. The street that used to connect to old Poletown to the south has been obliterated. Now, only the low, flat building of the Cadillac plant can be seen just above the berms and past the railroad tracks.

The Café India Restaurant and Coney Island reflect the new blending of cultures in Hamtramck.

143

This is one of the last vestiges of Dodge Main—one of the employee parking lot signs on Conant

By 1990, Mayor Robert Kozaren was a fixture in Hamtramck. In many ways, he loomed just as large as Dodge Main had in representing the city. But while he provided a degree of stability, Hamtramck was changing in many other ways, some rather curious. What once had been the Polish Falcons hall quietly converted into a rock club called Motor. Not far away, on Jos. Campau near Casmere, the Attic bar established itself as one of the finest blues bars in the state. Carbon, another club across the street, opened as well. Farther south, Lush moved into the old All American bar. Lilly's developed a reputation as the best hard rock bar in the metro Detroit area. The fact that it was located in a cramped old building on a side street off Jos. Campau only seemed to make it more attractive to the patrons. These new clubs complemented familiar nightspots such as Paychecks Lounge, Senate Café, and New Dodge Bar. Bars had always been a part of Hamtramck's social scene, but most were the corner shot-and-a-beer watering holes where people played pool and solved the problems of the world. This new breed of bars, which attracted the likes of flamboyant rocker Boy George, who served as a guest disk jockey at Motor one night in 2000, would have baffled the drinkers of yore.

Hamtramck had become trendy. In fact, the *Utne Reader*, an alternative culture magazine, named Hamtramck as one of the "hippest cities in America." It was even hip in a traditional way. Resident Leon Zarski won two Grammy awards for traditional polkas he wrote.

Still, the city's image was changing, and helping that was a growing artist community, attracted by the low rents and homey yet intensely urban atmosphere that Hamtramck provides. Some likened Hamtramck to New York City on a small scale with touches of a European city. It was precisely that type of atmosphere that brought Charles Cergenski and Janine Menlove to Hamtramck. They opened the Zone V film company in a storefront of Jos. Campau. Zone V specializes in locally produced non-exploitation films, such as *Stardust*, a sweet story of a vacuum cleaner that comes to life.

The attributes that made Hamtramck an attractive place to live seven decades ago—its walkability, central location, low cost of living, and close neighborhoods—were still intact as the new century approached. Along with the artists, a new generation of professional people moved into town, including college professors, businesspersons, engineers, and newspaper reporters. Often, many new residents were native Hamtramckans, those returning to the city after having moved away. Non-immigrant newcomers also moved in. Some arrived from such upscale communities as Royal Oak and even Birmingham, which are excellent, but expensive, communities in which to live.

Corresponding with the growth of the community was a rise in property values. Homes that sold for as little as $17,000 in 1988 were being marketed at $65,000 in 2000. As with the boost in population growth, Hamtramck's housing values showed the highest increase in Wayne County.

The newcomers, both from overseas and the other side of Eight Mile Road, had at first a subtle impact on Hamtramck. That began to change as they became more politically active, just as previous generations of immigrants had done. Kozaren had faced little more than token challenges through the 1980s and into the 1990s, but by 1993, the administration began to fray at the edges in the same way that the city's appearance was getting raggedy. Hamtramck once prided itself on its clean appearance, but by the 1990s the city was becoming inundated with litter. This was particularly unacceptable to the new residents who moved to town from other suburban communities that routinely provided street sweeping.

Hamtramck had long since given up such amenities in budget cutting moves. In 1993, former Department of Public Works superintendent Michael Niziol mounted a strong campaign against Kozaren. Although Kozaren easily won re-election, the challenge was a clear sign that there were growing feelings of dissatisfaction among the residents. Two years later, in 1995, Kozaren found himself in the first real battle for re-election in his entire tenure as mayor. Councilman Paul Odrobina, who had been on the city council during the critical years when the GM plant proposal was being implemented, also had broad support across the city. Given Kozaren's strength over the years, it was stunning when Odrobina came within 101 votes of Kozaren's total: 1,902 to 1,801. Clearly, Kozaren was in trouble. Hamtramck was approaching the twenty-first century, but in many ways, the city was stagnating. There were few examples of significant development. The Hamtramck Town Center and Senior Citizen Plaza, both on the R-31 land, were exceptions, but just across the street, the Holbrook-Caniff building, one of the most significant architectural examples in the city, was demolished after a fire. However, many people felt that it could have, and should have, been saved.

Increasingly, it seemed that Kozaren was losing touch with the people who had supported him for more than a decade. Every year, he had provided the impetus for the popular annual city festival, but just as the Romans of old learned, distractions don't solve fundamental problems. The year 1997 was also the city's 75th anniversary year, and a variety of events had been planned, including a special banquet in November, although there would be no dancing in the streets as there had been for the 50th anniversary in 1972. It was a pivotal year for Kozaren and the city. He had been beset by a host of problems, some relating to the city festival, which attracted the attention of the Internal Revenue Service. Although there were no substantial findings of wrongdoing, the problems preoccupied his administration. As the summer progressed, there was speculation on how he would fare in the upcoming election.

That may have been the topic of someone's interrupted conversation at 6:15 p.m. on Wednesday, July 2, when politics suddenly became inconsequential. It had been a hot and humid day, and storm clouds gathered in the steamy weather. Late in the afternoon, the sky turned to a nearly impenetrable black and the winds began to roar. A tornado was sweeping though the city. It had entered from the northwest, having passed through Detroit and Highland Park, and cut across

Mayor Robert Kozaren meets the media in 1995 near the end of his long tenure. (Courtesy of The Citizen.*)*

The tornado cut a path of destruction diagonally across the city.

Caniff to Conant, then south, and back into Detroit. Its passage took only minutes, but they were devastating ones. Houses began to sway, roofs were sent flying, and trees by the hundreds were uprooted. The super winds, which were clocked at 184 miles per hour, ripped off the facades of storefronts along the tornado's path. Whole buildings were crushed. Kanas Hall, the site of innumerable political rallies, parties and banquets for decades, was torn apart. Farther south on Conant, the Knights of Columbus Hall was also severely hurt, but would recover. The Allen Lumber Company, at Holbrook and Caniff, was not so fortunate. It felt the direct impact of the tornado and was completely leveled.

In minutes, Hamtramck was transformed into what looked like a war zone. The uprooted trees crushed cars and blocked streets, making some completely impassible. Many power lines were down, and some were live. With the streets flooded by the torrential rain, the power lines posed a potentially fatal hazard. There was also the threat of fire, which could have been more devastating than the tornado. No emergency vehicles could move down the blocked streets, and with the houses so close to one another, a fire could have turned into an inferno. Police, fire, and emergency crews from around southeastern Michigan began to arrive quickly. Tree removal services brought in equipment from as far away as Georgia to deal with the debris. Police sealed off the entrances to the city to all except residents and emergency personnel. That night, along the path of the tornado, was one of the darkest and quietest in the city's history. Power would not be restored to some areas until the following Monday. The steamy July heat settled over the streets like a curtain and the silence was complete. There were no televisions blaring, and the always-present background noise of passing cars was absent. The peace was welcomed compared to the carnage earlier that day. Cleanup operations began by the next day as the sound of chainsaws set the tone for the whole city. Many trees had uprooted sidewalks as they fell, and these all had to be cleared. Miraculously, no one had been killed by the tornado. Only one man would die, of a heart attack, while cleaning up the debris.

A month later, just scars would remain. Some damaged buildings were still being repaired and many trees that survived the storm were badly disfigured and left with oddly shaped tops where their trunks and branches had been snapped. They would serve as reminders of the devastation for years.

Residents took note of the quick response the city made to the disaster, both in calling for help and mobilizing resources to repair the damage. Kozaren could take pride in what he had accomplished and in showing that he was capable of acting decisively, but while it may not have been too little, it definitely was too late. A new political star was on the rise. Gary Zych had virtually come out of nowhere, politically, to be elected to the city council two years earlier. Indeed, he had garnered enough votes to win the top spot as council president. He ran a classic grassroots campaign, going door to door, personally meeting as many people as he could. While Kozaren had relied on his cast of longtime supporters, Zych was reaching out to the new generation of Hamtramckans, an effective way of building support. It also helped define the distinctly growing lines that would pit "old" Hamtramck against "new" Hamtramck.

Zych's grandparents had owned property in Hamtramck, but he grew up in East Detroit (later named Eastpointe). His father, Edward, was a member of St.

Massive trees were uprooted and crushed cars by the dozens in the few minutes it took the tornado to pass on one afternoon in July 1997.

148

Florian parish and would bring Zych, as a boy, into town, leaving him with lasting memories of the city. Later, Zych graduated from Notre Dame High School and received a degree in fine arts from the University of Michigan. He also taught with the Grosse Pointe Schools.

While an undergraduate student, he met some students who lived in Hamtramck. That sparked Zych to take a renewed interest in the town. He moved to Hamtramck in the 1980s and bought a building, which he converted into an art studio. "I was subconsciously getting back to my roots," he recalled. Plus, he appreciated what Hamtramck had to offer. "It has a sense of place, a sense of social atmosphere. I felt it was a community that was walkable and with a lot of character."

Zych got to know some of the politicians in town and began to take an interest in local politics. He also got to see the city's failings and how its character was being threatened by losses that weren't being replaced, such as the demolition of the history-laden Martha Washington Theatre, which was used as the site for a fast food restaurant.

Zych taught at Lawrence Technological University in Southfield. That alone made him suspect in the eyes of some of the city's old guard. Zych wasn't alone in that position. Other political newcomers were being branded as arrogant pseudo-intellectuals who felt they knew how to run the city better because they had college degrees. There may have been some truth to that impression, but it was just a perception, a generality that missed the whole picture. Whatever the case, Zych faced a rocky two years on the city council that would often turn into a hostile arena of confrontations. The division between the old guard politicians and newcomers was splitting the voters almost exactly down the middle. In the November 1997 election, Zych slipped by Kozaren by a razor-thin margin of nine votes. Kozaren called for a recount, but that only confirmed the numbers. "It's time for the mayor to move on. It's overdue," Zych said during the recount.

That's exactly what Kozaren did, bringing to a close the longest-serving administration in the city's history. It is not easy to assess the administration of Mayor Kozaren. In many ways, he represented the best of Hamtramck. Tough, resourceful, optimistic, he always maintained a deep commitment to the city. He was not single-handedly responsible for bringing the GM plant to Hamtramck, but he played a pivotal role as a negotiator who was able to sell the idea to all facets of the community. GM and Detroit were in no mood to become entangled in local politics and could have gone elsewhere to locate the factory. Kozaren kept everyone on the same track locally while Detroit, state, federal, and GM officials carried out the complex details.

He was exactly the right person in office at the time when Hamtramck needed a dynamic leader who could appreciate the opportunity he faced. He met the challenge. He also built on the city's strengths with the creation of the annual city festival and other programs. But Kozaren stepped into the trap that many very long-serving politicians do: he became increasingly isolated and unreceptive to the people. His world closed in too tightly around his office in city hall. Ironically, he began to develop the attitude that had doomed his predecessor. He lost his enthusiasm, perhaps without even realizing it.

Despite that, Kozaren stands as tall historically as he did physically in Hamtramck's story. His record tenure, the city festival, and even his deep faith in the city made a lasting impact. Plus, the role he played in bringing the GM plant to Hamtramck was instrumental. In that critical period, he accomplished what seemed to be impossible in Hamtramck. He got everyone to put aside their personal feelings and work together for the good of Hamtramck.

In January of 1998, it became Zych's opportunity to create a legacy as he moved into city hall. He immediately began making changes, starting with a thorough overhaul of what had been Kozaren's office for 18 years. Kozaren, a heavy smoker, had left the office permeated with cigarette smoke, which Zych made into an object lesson of cleaning it for the new administration. Some interpreted the action as disrespectful to the man many perceived as having saved Hamtramck, but Zych was not going to stand in Kozaren's shadow. He had his own ideas on what Hamtramck needed and wanted to implement them. Moribund city commissions were reactivated and new ones established, such as the Historical Commission, the Beautification Commission, the Plan Commission, and the Human Relations Commission. The latter was charged with helping the city deal with the rapidly diversifying makeup of the populace, since while the city was firmly in the hands of Polish-American administrators, the majority of the population no longer was of Polish descent.

Today, only about 38 percent of the students in the Hamtramck public schools speak English as their primary language. Rather, you will often hear Arabic, Bulgarian, Bosnian, Somali, Ukrainian, Urdu, Romanian, German, Punjabi, Albanian, Russian, Spanish, Bengali, Serbo-Croatian, and Polish. Just how many students this diversity represents is shown in the school-by-school breakdown. Dickinson West Elementary School has the highest percentage of students who speak English as a first language—a mere 40 percent. Superintendent Keyworth could appreciate the challenge facing Hamtramck educators today.

Signs of assimilation are evident all around town. Just as happened decades ago, it's not unusual to see a small child interpreting for his or her parents at a store where they are buying something. As happens in so many ways, the children are leading the way. They are bringing English into the homes and introducing American ways to their families. There is some resistance as not every American custom is welcome in some homes, but the change is inevitable. Traditional dress of the old homeland is usually shed in favor of jeans fairly quickly, and few teens of any nationality can resist the charm—such as it is—of the shopping malls.

The new immigrants, however, have yet to make a significant impact on the political scene, although Arab and other Islamic community members did support Zych. A few non-Poles have run for office, but none as yet have been elected. In that sense, the new immigrants have not paralleled the history of the Poles, who quickly adapted to and learned the ways of United States democracy. But time will show if that will change, and it most likely will.

For the present, Hamtramck politics remain traditionally hostile as Mayor Zych quickly learned once in office. He immediately faced opposition from the council and a variety of others in and out of city hall. He was subjected to two recall votes, and survived them both. He attempted to make some radical changes in city operations, including privatizing some city services, and ran into some opposition. Foes claimed he was arrogant, rude, and crude. He certainly could play political hardball with the most veteran politicians, and the attitude he directed at some city hall employees deeply offended them, turning them into bitter political enemies, who gladly supported the recall efforts.

Conversely, Zych was trying to build some bridges with Washington, D.C., and especially with Wayne County, which had the resources to help the city. Working with the city's Downtown Development Authority, the city was able to win a $2.5-million grant to redevelop the Jos. Campau strip between Holbrook and Caniff. Decorative sidewalks and street lamps were to be installed, which would replace the sidewalks and lamps installed more than 20 years earlier when the city was seeking to revitalize itself in the wake of the closing of Dodge Main. Part of the project also included a complete renovation of the city's main parking lot off

Hamtramck's new diversity is apparent in abundance as Mayor Gary Zych meets with some kids at the park.

Mayor Gary Zych meets with President Clinton during one of Zych's visits to Washington, D.C.

Jos. Campau, a lot that has been neglected for years. The project was shaping up as being one of the most significant in decades and one of the largest public improvements in the city's history. And it was on track for a June 2002 launch.

Zych also worked behind the scenes to at last bring to an end the three-decade-old urban renewal case. He flew to Washington, D.C. twice, at his own expense, to meet with federal officials, including Andrew Cuomo, secretary of the Department of Housing and Urban Development, and ultimately crafted a redevelopment plan. The proposal, which was agreed to by all parties in the case, including Judge Damon Keith, will provide new houses and establish funding to rebuild sewers and streets in the Dyar–Grand Haven area. Zych also worked diligently to push a $4.3-million lawsuit against Sherwin Williams Company, over the contamination of the old Acme paint company site.

But all was not well in Hamtramck, by far. On the political front, Zych was nearing the end of his first term in office and the city was facing a $2.9-million deficit, partially due to a $2.1-million arbitration award received by the city's police officers. However, the budget problems went deeper than that. The city was faced with rising personnel costs, and there had been talk among some officials that the city's workforce was too large. Yet, prospects of layoffs were met with opposition. Zych wanted to privatize trash services, as most other Michigan communities have done, but again, that was protested by city workers. When

Zych and the council could not agree on a budget, the state stepped in once again. On August 3, 2001, the state warned that it would invoke Public Act 72 of 1990 to take over the city if it did not present a balanced budget with a deficit reduction plan by October 1. The council was split, with three members opposing Zych's proposals and two in favor. Neither side would budge.

On October 24, Frederick Headen of the State Department of Treasury wrote to the city council warning, "The State of Michigan has grave doubts concerning both the capacity and willingness of city officials to address the city's financial problems . . . the fact that this opportunity has not been utilized by city officials will . . . leave the state little option but to pursue a takeover."

When that failed to move the problem off center, the state made good on its threat and announced that it was sending emergency financial manager Louis Schimmel to take over Hamtramck's finances in November. Schimmel was a no-nonsense Republican from Waterford Township who focused squarely on the bottom line. One of his first acts was to eliminate the $12,000 annual salaries of the council members and the mayor's $20,000 salary. He told the council not to bother meeting anymore because he was making all the decisions, although they did begin meeting anyway after a short suspension. He then promptly pronounced the city's financial books a mess and started on a course of cost cutting. In short order he privatized the city's trash pickup, as Zych had tried to do, and solved the city's most pressing problem—the accumulation of trash that had occurred because of a DPW slowdown. Under the threat of payless paydays and a proposal to replace the city's police with patrols by the Wayne County Sheriff's Department, Schimmel renegotiated contracts with the city employees and gradually began to bring the city's finances more in line. Nothing was off the table in front of Schimmel. Dissatisfied with the condition of city hall, he announced a plan to close the building and move operations to the Department of Public Works building. The proposal drew strong protests from some residents, many of whom had been born in the building when it had been St. Francis Hospital. Ultimately the plan to renovate the Department of Public Works building proved too costly and was dropped.

These acts and Schimmel's "my way or the highway" approach made it perfectly clear that he was the boss. This did not sit well with critics, who challenged his authority in some matters. For instance, Schimmel got involved in making appointments to the city's Housing Commission. That program is funded by the federal government so it does not directly involve city money, over which Schimmel did have jurisdiction. But Schimmel had circumstances and a "Catch 22" situation working in his favor. The only way to truly challenge Schimmel's authority was to test Public Act 72 in court. But Schimmel controlled the city's money, and he wasn't about to authorize a potentially lengthy and expensive lawsuit against himself. Despite the way some people viewed him, Schimmel wasn't blindly unreasonable. And while he coldly eyed the bottom line, that is exactly what he needed to do if the city's finances were to be straightened out.

And the garbage was being picked up again.

It is one of the greatest ironies of the history of Hamtramck that it was taken over by a Republican who brought order to the city's chaotic finances. Realistically, Schimmel is not going to be remembered fondly by most Hamtramckans. To them, he was a high-handed state appointee who represented the very antithesis of Democracy—taxation without representation. His $100,000-a-year salary was being paid by the Hamtramckans, but they could not remove him from office, nor was he in any way accountable to the people of Hamtramck. He was only answerable to the State Treasury Department. And the folks in Lansing did not care what he did, so long as Hamtramck's books were balanced.

So, Schimmel was insulated from the resentment and did not have to react to the protests when he canceled the popular city festival after the Chamber of Commerce was unable to assume control. However, Schimmel was not insensitive to the feelings of Hamtramckans. In November 2001, he published his own community newsletter, called *Hurrah Hamtramck*. In it, he outlined the city's problems and what he had been doing to correct them and he laid the responsibility for the city's predicament squarely on the local politicians. "I blame the sorry state of Hamtramck on feuding politicians," he wrote. "The elected officials were so embroiled in controversies they did not pay attention to the business at hand."

But Schimmel didn't help his bid for understanding by having the newsletter produced by a company in Grosse Pointe, which is a long way from Hamtramck. In fact, by the time it was distributed door to door, a good portion of the information already was out of date because plans had changed.

State emergency financial manager Louis Schimmel addresses the public in the city council chambers. In the background is Councilman John Justewicz. (Courtesy of The Citizen.*)*

Despite the fact that the city officials had been stripped of their power and most had lost their paychecks, a host of candidates lined up to run for office in the September 2001 primary. Seven people joined the race for mayor, 15 for five spots on the city council, and three were seeking to become city clerk.

Zych squared off against city clerk Ethel Fiddler, who had become a bitter foe of the mayor. The election results were exceptionally close—Zych won by five votes, 1,655 to 1,650. A recount was inevitable, but Zych prevailed by a mere two votes. It was hardly a mandate of the people, but three supporters of Zych were elected to the council, setting the stage, at least, for less rancorous council meetings and a break in the gridlock that had paralyzed the administration.

To the average Hamtramckan, the happenings in city hall were of little interest. What they were most concerned with were the quality of life issues: that the trash was picked up and city services were offered. And as Hamtramck moved into the twenty-first century, that was the state of the city. It remained a ragged, gritty town that still had one foot in the grime of the old factories and another in the computer age. At worst, it could be said that the city was not going backward. Even the financial crisis that brought state intervention was more of a sign of the city's cantankerous political scene than a fundamental failing. Schimmel was perceptive in identifying the source of Hamtramck's woes. As they did nearly a century before, the politicians split into camps and battled each other, much to the detriment of the city.

Is that likely to change? No. If anything, the political scene has become even more dysfunctional in recent years.

Will that doom the city? No. As was stated before, Hamtramck survives in spite of itself. It has a core resiliency that continues to give the city the bounce it needs to keep coming back from each crisis. There are, in fact, many encouraging signs that the city is well positioned for the future. The population continues to grow, property values are rising, and the key indicators of the city's real strength are positive. Those indicators are not found in the city's budget: they are found in the homeowner who builds a garage next to his house, the person who strips off the old plywood front of a former corner store and restores the beautiful glass block wall beneath. They are found in the businesses that give the town a special character, such as the Urban Break coffee house, Salvador Deli, both of which host poetry readings and art programs, as well as the old Polish bakeries and meat markets and the new Indian and Bangladeshi stores. They are found in the thriving public library that operates a host of programs that belies its small size. And they are found in the community amenities, such as the Planet Ant live theater and the numerous clubs. They are found in volunteers who devote their time to boards and commissions. These are signs that people still care about their town and are willing to support it. The residents' willingness to tax themselves to support a recreation program is just one indication of that care.

And there is plenty of life in the town. Just walk down Jos. Campau on a Saturday. The sidewalks are packed. Or try to maneuver through the crush of traffic. And remember that while drivers may creep along the streets clogged with traffic on a Saturday afternoon in Hamtramck, cars breeze down the far larger but often vacant Woodward Avenue in downtown Detroit. The streets are like long thermometers. The higher the numbers of cars, the hotter the town is.

Of course the city will change in the years ahead. The decades of Polish prominence are probably over for good, although a new influx of Poles is taking place as well. But it's difficult to imagine that it will approach the numbers of the past. More Arabs and Bosnians or African Americans or Bangladeshis, or any others in the spectrum of the cultures present, will get more politically involved and take their place in city hall. To the city's great credit, all are being encouraged to participate in the community. The city seems to have learned some bitter lessons from the abysmal treatment of the African-American residents in the old urban renewal case and operations of the housing project.

Already, neighbors of different cultures are crossing the barriers that separate them. They're speaking over fences, although often in broken English, to share their concerns. And maybe a favorite family dish. Haline Piechota of Wyandotte Street took the children of her Yemeni neighbors to a community event at the park. Little things make a difference. Barriers do crumble.

Where Hamtramck is today was shown five days after the September 11, 2001 terrorist attacks. A multi-cultural ceremony was held at Veterans Memorial Park that brought together ministers, priests, imams, and several hundred residents in a show of unity and understanding. Seldom has the city collectively stood so proudly.

Where it will be in the future is shown by the census trends. "We will experience a moderate continued growth for at least five years," Mayor Zych predicted. He plans to expand the city's contacts with other government entities and bring the city's operations into a more modern mode. The archaic city charter, which is built on a framework written in 1922, is under review to be revised and updated. More emphasis is being placed on those quality-of-life issues that were often ignored in the past, like zoning restrictions, building codes, and the enforcement of city ordinances.

Hamtramck's problems will never be solved. What city's problems are? Almost assuredly the state will intervene in the city's operations again some day. That seems to be a natural order of life in Hamtramck. But when it does, the city will get back on track and overcome whatever problem it is facing at that time and go on. Political bickering will continue and inevitably mistakes will be made, opportunities will be missed, and decay will occur, even as restoration takes place.

That's part of life in the city and the life of the city. But indications are that Hamtramck will continue to defy the odds that have condemned so many inner city neighborhoods to inevitable decline. Whatever happens, Hamtramck somehow always manages to prevail.

And so it goes . . .

BIBLIOGRAPHY

Babson, Peter. *Working Detroit: The Making of a Union Town*. Detroit: Wayne State University Press, 1986.

Blum, Peter H. *Brewed in Detroit: Breweries and Beers Since 1830*. Detroit: Wayne State University Press, 1999.

Cohen, Irwin. *Echoes of Detroit*. Haslett: City Vision Publishing, 2000.

Kavieff, Paul R. *The Violent Years*. Fort Lee: Barricade Books, 2001.

King, Donald E. *Arrivederci, Hurley—Halo, Hamtramck*. New York: Vantage Press, 1992.

Kowalski, Greg; Charlene Sloan; and Joseph Sobota. *Our Town*. Hamtramck: Hamtramck 75th Anniversary committee, 1997.

Marsh, Harriet. *History of Detroit*. Crawfordsville: The Lakeside Press, E.R. Donnelley & Sons, 1935.

May, George S. *Michigan, An Illustrated History of the Great Lakes State*. Northridge: Windsor Publications Inc., 1987.

Morrison, Andre Craig. *Opera House, Nickel Show, and Palace*. Dearborn: Greenfield Village and Henry Ford Museum, 1974.

Otten, William L. *Col. J.F. Hamtramck, His Life and Times (1756-1783)*. Port Arkansas, Texas: William Otten Jr., 1997.

Pittrone, Jean Maddern. *Tangled Web: Legacy of Auto Pioneer, John F. Dodge*. Hamtramck: Avenue Publishing Company, 1989.

Plumb, Mildred. *History of Tau Beta*. Detroit: Evans-Winter-Hebb Inc., 1938.

Radzilowski, Thaddeus. *The Polish Experience in Detroit*. Detroit: Detroit Historical Museum, 2001.

Rarogiewicz, E.W. *Hamtramck Yearbook—1947–1948*. Hamtramck: E.W. Rarogiewicz, 1948.

Schrode, Georg. *Polonia's Working-Class People and Local Politics*. Unpublished master's thesis, 1985.

Serafino, Frank. *West of Warsaw*. Hamtramck: Avenue Publishing Company, 1983.

St. Florian Parish. *Golden Jubilee Memories*. Hamtramck: 1958.

Wood, Arthur Evans. *Hamtramck, Then and Now*. New York: Octagon Books, 1956.

Writers of the Works Projects Administration. *Michigan: A Guide to the Wolverine State*. New York: Oxford University Press, 1941.

Newspapers:
Virtually all copies of the *Plain Dealer* from 1934 to 1950 were used as reference, as were all copies of *The Citizen* from 1950 to February 2002.

A group of children play at Holbrook Elementary School. The school has been in continuous use since 1896, although the original building was a wooden structure. The school reflects the changing ethnicity of the city, as almost all the children are Muslim.

INDEX